Pakistan: Another Vision

Fifty years of painting and sculpture from Pakistan

D1438595

Pakistan
Another Vision

Fifty Years of Painting and Sculpture from Pakistan

Edited by **Timothy Wilcox**

Published on the occasion of the exhibition
Pakistan: Another Vision

Presented by **Asia House** and
Arts & The Islamic World

Brunei Gallery
School of Oriental and
African Studies, London

12 April – 18 June 2000
Huddersfield Art Gallery
23 June – 5 August 2000

Oldham Art Gallery
12 August – 9 September 2000

Victoria Art Gallery, Bath
Hot Bath Gallery, Bath
19 September – 8 November 2000

Lead sponsors
American Express Bank Ltd.
Pakistan International Airlines
Shell Pakistan Limited
American Express Bank Ltd.
is regulated by the SFA

Sponsors
Babar Ali Foundation
Crescent Group
Dawn Group of Newspapers
Hascombe Ltd
International General Insurance Company of Pakistan Limited
Marriott Hotels
Darayus Happy Minwalla
United Bank Limited
The VM Gallery
and anonymous benefactors

The exhibition is supported by
the Pakistan National Council of the Arts

Published by
Arts & The Islamic World (UK) Ltd
16 Grosvenor Crescent
London SW1X 7EP

ISBN 1-903411-00-9

Images © the artists or artists' estates
Texts © the authors 2000
Photography by: Nasim Akhtar, Lahore;
Zahoor Ahmed, Karachi; Fon Hutacharern, London

Cat **12**, **13** by permission Shakir Ali Museum, Lahore
Cat **21**, **22** by permission Chughtai Museum, Lahore

Catalogue designed by Graphic Ideas
Catalogue printed by Hastings Printing Company

Front cover: **77 Anwar Saeed** *Love is a Lungfish I* 1992
Frontispiece: **95 Anwar Jalal Shemza** *The Wall* 1958
Back cover: **65 Mohammed Imran Qureshi** *A Lover waiting for his Beloved* 1999

Contents

22 Abdur Rahman Chughtai *A Poet with Song Birds* c.1955

Introduction

Pakistan: Another Vision is the first exhibition to look historically at the art of Pakistan since Independence in 1947. Pakistan has been host to many ancient civilisations: the Indus Valley civilisation of Moenjodaro and Harappa, the Graeco-Buddhist civilisation at Taxila and the North West Frontier, and the many Muslim kingdoms whose buildings can be found in Punjab and Sindh, particularly the Mughal monuments in Lahore. What is much less well known is the energy and vision of the country's contemporary artists, who over a period of more than fifty years have given concrete expression to the aspirations, and trials, of the emerging nation. While individual artists or small groups have been exhibited internationally, at the Venice Biennale, Sao Paolo, Fukuoka or Brisbane, there has been no attempt until now to survey the whole spectrum of Pakistan's art in Britain, nor to present current production in the context of earlier work. This exhibition is evidence not only of the great wealth and diversity of art in Pakistan, but of the artists' ambitions to make art that is relevant and meaningful, not only within the country itself, but for today's global community.

The exhibition is presented by Asia House in partnership with *Arts & The Islamic World*. It has benefited throughout from the support of the Pakistan National Council for the Arts, and its Director General, Ghulam Rasul. The original concept was that of Sir Nicholas Barrington, formerly High Commissioner in Pakistan and member of Asia House's Executive Committee, who has taken a leading role in bringing together the many parties involved in the realisation of this complex project.

We are honoured to acknowledge the patronage of the exhibition by the Pakistan High Commissioner in London and the British High Commissioner in Islamabad. The exhibition has also benefited from the London Advisory Committee under the chairmanship of Sir Nicholas Barrington, in particular the contribution of Mumtaz Khan; the support of the Chairman of the Asia House Pakistan Committee, F S Aijazuddin, and an informal group of artists and critics in Pakistan, whose contribution has been invaluable. We wish to thank Katriana Hazell, Cultural Director of Asia House and Thea Evans, Cultural Assistant for their work co-ordinating the exhibition, and of course the indefatigable curator Timothy Wilcox.

Without the support of its generous sponsors, listed elsewhere in this publication, the exhibition could not have been realised. We are immensely grateful to them all. Finally we express our gratitude to all the artists and lenders, especially as most of the paintings and sculptures shown here have never before been seen outside Pakistan. Their whole-hearted commitment to this enterprise is warmly acknowledged.

Sir Peter Wakefield
Chairman
Asia House

Jalal Uddin Ahmed
Roving Editor
Arts & The Islamic World

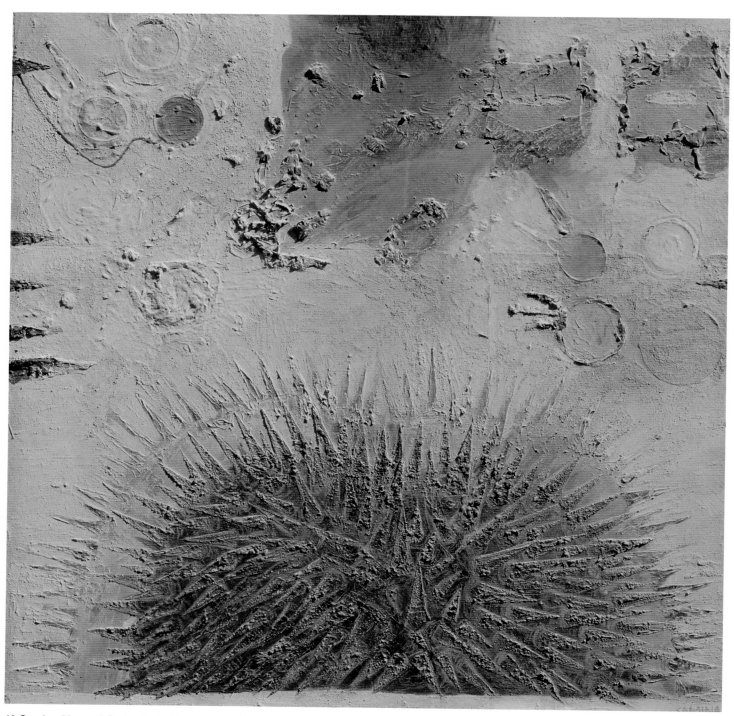

42 Samina Mansuri *Raging Eye* 1993

Modern Art in Pakistan

It took a German, Nikolaus Pevsner, to attempt to probe the national character of the English as revealed in their culture, coining in the process his unforgettable phrase, 'The Englishness of English Art'. Given as the BBC Reith Lectures in 1955, Pevsner's analysis belongs to a period of post-war optimism and reconciliation; though hotly debated ever since, his endeavour has remained a touchstone in any discussion of national identity, cultural stereotypes and international understanding.

At the dawn of a new century, as the first-ever historical survey of the visual art of Pakistan is presented in London, there is, understandably, a sense of anticipation, but qualified now with some scepticism: is there also a '-ness' to the art of Pakistan? With more than one hundred works in the exhibition, much will be revealed of the artists' ways of shaping and expressing their environment, personal, social and political. How will these individual works contribute to the different understandings of the nation or its culture for any of the various audiences the exhibition will attract?

Pevsner's title was calculated to excite the interest of the British art establishment at a time when modern art was becoming increasingly international, not only in its ambition, but in its execution and delivery. Modernism had become a global 'lingua franca', applicable in any situation, and disdained such incidental obstacles as geography or economics. The greatness of any work of art was to be judged precisely by the absence of any specific reference to time or place. What Rothko exemplified in painting was demonstrated even more pertinently by Le Corbusier's designs for Chandigarh, the new capital of the Indian state of Punjab, created after the previous capital, Lahore, became part of Pakistan. Despite its arcades for shade and its water channels, the new city made very few concessions to the Indian climate or way of life.

The idea, widely held in the fifties and sixties, that the work of art can transcend any specific national or historical context has since been challenged from many different perspectives. If the universality claimed for modernist art has little credence today, what is to replace it? It is clear there can be no single answer; and if the lack of a unified discourse implies a plurality, this is a plurality which will change its character radically, not only from place to place or from age to age, but from individual to individual. In the absence of a 'one size fits all' aesthetic, how do we judge what the artist means by wearing a three-piece

suit, or jeans or 'shalwaar kameez'? The answer will be different in Bond Street or in Schon Circle, Karachi. One of the reasons why the art of Pakistan deserves greater international attention is the sheer complexity of the tangled strands of which it is formed. The use of other metaphorical terms like 'interwoven' or 'multilayered' for this plurality have to be rejected, as the degree of structural organisation they imply seems hardly appropriate to the actual situation.

Viewing the art of Pakistan 'in context' is not as easy as it sounds, however. There are simply too many different ways of imagining what the relevant context might be. This essay suggests some – religious, political, feminist – all to a greater or lesser degree interrelated and overlapping. Many of the works selected for the exhibition relate directly to ideas of place - sometimes very specifically, sometimes only generally or metaphorically. It cannot be said that they add up to a general statement about Pakistan or its art, only that there are many approaches; and when the art from one country is transplanted and shown in another, the sense of place is not something to be taken for granted, but something worth interrogating. This is one of the things the exhibition sets out to do. The context in which the art is seen thus has a physical, space-time dimension too; the self-same works would have had quite a different impact if they were to be shown together in Pakistan.

Setting aside the international focus, and trying to think of the art from the local perspective of Pakistan raises more questions than it answers. Should the mental construct we might call 'local context' embrace the whole country and its population? Or can the art only be properly understood in relation to conditions in the regional centres of Karachi, Lahore, Peshawar or Quetta? Narrowing the focus still further, is the true environment of the production and consumption of art more correctly envisaged as a sector of the wealthy, well educated English-speaking society in certain suburbs of Lahore or the glamourous but heartless developments of the Defence Housing Association in Karachi? These questions are certainly relevant in London, because they condition the way certain artists live and work in Pakistan; for some, the existence of a well-established market has meant that they have worked for up to twenty years without needing to submit themselves or their work to the scrutiny of public exhibition; in so doing they have avoided both unsympathetic comment and also the benefits of informed criticism. Artists of the younger

13 Shakir Ali *Woman with Birdcage* 1968

generation, especially in Karachi, but also, to a lesser extent, in Lahore, have taken the need to find less exclusive audiences as a major premise for their activity.

The state of Pakistan was founded in 1947 by the Act of Partition. The new nation, with a name meaning 'Land of the Pure' grew out of the aspiration for an Islamic state distinct from Hindu-dominated India. Consisting initially of East and West Pakistan, the country divided when the eastern part declared independence in 1972 and became Bangladesh. Unlike many countries emerging from colonial rule, where the indigenous culture went through a process of reassessment and re-evaluation and adapted over a period of time to the new circumstances of independence, in Pakistan the Islamic allegiance to which the state owed its very existence seemed to provide a ready-made culture. The poetry of Iqbal and the paintings of **Chughtai** were living testimony to the vibrancy of this ideal. When the Lahore Arts Council reopened its galleries in 1948 after the unrest of partition Chughtai was celebrated as the founder of a new national school. Due to the pain of recent events, the status he enjoyed in pre-independence India now counted for far less than the endorsements of critics and curators in Britain. His reputation at home was inseparable from his success abroad, as the extract from the 1954 book *Art in Pakistan* makes plain. So although visually his art proclaimed a clear adherence to a specifically Islamic heritage – and saw its role as a duty to isolate those elements from other traditions in the sub-continent – there were aspects of Chughtai's activity where the focus was not local at all, but international. The two works included here were selected, in part, because they were exhibited in Paris in the 1950s. Pakistan's art was not founded on a simple dialectic of the national versus the international, the traditional versus the modern. Artists were engaged in all these areas and often chose not to resolve opposites but to maintain a tension – which existed in many other areas of life – by playing one off against the other.

In practice, the modern art of Pakistan is by no means circumscribed by Islam. It may even be true to say that Islam is not actually dominant among the five or six major traditions which are entwined in the country's present visual culture. The situation is nonetheless very different from the secularism of Euramerica (as 'the West' is now more appropriately termed from the Asian perspective), and religious sensibility is far from incompatible with artistic endeavour. In the hands of certain artists – **Sadequain, Shemza** or **Zahoor** – the arts and ideology of Islam have underpinned and sustained the creativity of an entire career. The same could not, perhaps, be said of many artists of the younger generation.

In more than a century of cultural exchange between Euramerica and Asia, Euramerica has consistently projected its own desire for purity onto the 'exotic' culture, paying attention to it only so far as it met its (Euramerica's) need for the 'authentic', the 'primitive', the 'purely decorative'. The fact that the art of Pakistan is, on the contrary, so often equivocal, so often subversive of its own codes and the codes of others, has made it difficult to understand, still less accept. Yet as the Australian John Clark, the leading scholar in this field has observed: 'The inability of Euramerican rhetoric to find modern art in Asia intelligible is the very sign that its subversion will open up the discourse of modernity itself' (*Modernity in Asian Art*, p16). The work of the sculptor **Shahid Sajjad**, who has audaciously interrogated the notion of the primitive within the terms of the sub-continent, is unsettling wherever it is viewed from. **Anwar Saeed's** recent paintings locate 'the Other' not at any geographical or temporal distance, but within the self; and the very approachability of his figures belies the brutally frank, uncomfortable undercurrents he is seeking to lay bare.

Sajjad has spent many years in Japan as well as in Britain. For Pakistan, situated on the Western fringe of the continent, almost all of Asia is 'oriental'. Relations with its nearest neighbours to the East, India and Bangladesh, are no less delicate, no less demanding of careful negotiation, culturally speaking, than those with Britain or the USA. Almost all the artists represented in this exhibition have spent time studying, or living abroad. If this community of artists is distinctly cosmopolitan, so too is its clientele. Certainly since the seventies, most of the gallery audience is well-travelled, and liberal-minded. While the aim of **Shakir Ali**, returning to Pakistan in 1951 from four years' study in Europe, may have been to forge a visual language which was meaningful to the newly autonomous nation of the fifties and sixties, later artists worked against a continuing background of open dialogue. References to Rothko, Newman, Hamilton or Bacon were made knowingly for an audience complicit in the activity of multi-cultural mobility.

In the 1960s, **Geoffrey**, **Parvez**, **Sadequain**, **Shemza** all received high-profile exhibitions in London or Paris. Europe (aware that it had lost the initiative to New York?) spoke of an

Fig **1 Khalid Iqbal** *Village Mosque* c.1970

Fig **2 Ustad Alla Bux** *Partition* c.1950

art which would marry East and West; on its own terms, of course. During the following decade the rise in economic power of the Gulf states and other developments in the Middle East left Euramerica less receptive to Islamic culture. Today's attitude is different again and could be called post-modern to the extent that it admits the co-existence of rival systems. Their mutual inter-dependence is triumphantly articulated in the work of **Shahzia Sikander**, but one wonders how many of the politicians moving up and down The Mall in Washington DC took time to notice, let alone reflect on, her recent extraordinary one-person show at the Hirshhorn Museum.

Sikander has travelled a long way from the miniature painter's studio in Lahore to the seat of government of the global superpower. Thanks to her, we realise how close these locations now are to each other. Her work is a compelling reflection of the sense of displacement engendered as artists and their work travel, together or separately, to different venues around the globe. The focus shifts from the familiar to the not-so-familiar, not simply in the collage of images, but in the value systems they represent. Sikander dramatises the simultaneous processes of gain and loss, forging a bond with the viewer and turning the apprehension of cultural difference into a shared experience. If issues alone made the art of an individual, or a people, significant (and there are some who would still echo Ruskin's dictum of 'the greatest number of the greatest ideas'), then Pakistan's would be among the most highly rated in the modern world. There is however no telescope – or video link – powerful enough to transmit to twenty-first-century England the explosive circumstances which left one artist holding a private view on a pavement, or which closed another's exhibition following a directive from the State Department; nor, for that matter, to explain the veneration in which the Lahore landscape painter **Khalid Iqbal** is truly held, by artists and collectors alike. The art of Pakistan makes its appeal to the intellect; it makes its appeal to the moral sense, the sense of justice and equality. Its greatest achievement, though, is not to be confined to those ends, but to go beyond them.

There are estimated to be around 1,000 artists making and exhibiting work in Pakistan. In a population of over 130 million, this is a very small number, but it is large in relation to the total of sixty-three who are included in this exhibition, not all of whom are still living. The selection, especially among the earlier artists, has been made not purely on historical grounds, but in order to highlight certain key themes which bear on current practice. In this process, certain artists who were undoubtedly of great significance in their day are not represented. By contrast, it seemed imperative to devote space to a number of rising talents, some of them not especially well established even within the country, but who provide at least a glimpse of a dynamic, exploratory attitude among the younger generation. Seven of these artists are under thirty. The remarks which follow concentrate on the artists and works in the exhibition. No attempt has been made to write a history of the art and artists of Pakistan. For this, the reader is referred to the publications in the **Resources** section on page 79.

In an important article entitled 'The Future of Art in Pakistan' which appeared in 1949, Chughtai laid out a personal manifesto for the new state: 'I regard it the duty of every artist to be fully conscious of his national traditions and through his consciousness influence others and prompt them to right action… In Pakistan we need an art which should reflect the individuality of the artist and be based on observations that conform to the highest artistic standards but which, at the same time, should depict the broad features of national life and be universal in its appeal' (quoted in M Nesom, *Abdur Rahman Chughtai: A Modern South Asian Artist*, dissertation, Ohio State University 1984, p344). From his earlier association with the artists of the Bengal School, Chughtai derived an understanding of the role art could play in the propagation of nationalist ideals. The illustrated books that he published reveal his desire to disseminate his work beyond the limited gallery audience. Lavishly produced, and not exactly accessible to the masses, they brought modern imagery to the literate, educated classes. The Urdu texts are in themselves an affirmation of national culture, but also reassert the interdependence of painting and writing which made the arts of the book one of the crowning achievements of the Muslim inheritance in the sub-continent. Chughtai's evanescent wash technique is, in part, a portrayal of the spirituality for which he strove, yet his chosen medium of watercolour on paper only served to distance him from the international modern tendency. Materials and techniques remain one of the prime areas of contention wherever identity is at issue. **Faiza Butt**, a recent student at the Slade School in London works with pen on paper, not because she does not know any better, as was implied to her by her tutors, but because she does; her choice of translucent inks and architect's film reveals an intimate engagement with the qualities of materials that embraces modernism's preoccupation with process only to withdraw from the clinch and seek a personal satisfaction elsewhere.

Fig **3 Murtaza Bashir** *Self-portrait* c.1956

The 1950s were a period of great ferment in the art, and the society, of Pakistan. The arrival of seven million refugees (and the departure of a similar number) in a country which waited until 1956 for a constitution seem inadequately represented by Chughtai's studious poets or dreamy princesses. Another artist with a pre-1947 reputation to rival Chughtai's, **Ustad Alla Bux** (1895-1978) painted *Partition* as a sea of humanity, but in an oblique visual language rooted in late nineteenth-century fantasy (fig **2**).

The figure who did most to establish international modernism as the central agenda for the country's art was **Shakir Ali**. Trained initially at the J J School of Art in Bombay, he arrived in Karachi via study at the Slade School in London, followed by a period with André Lhote, the codifier of cubism, in the South of France, and in Prague. A position at the Mayo School took him to Lahore in 1952 where he joined a lively group of artists and writers (often one and the same person) including **Shemza** and **Ahmed Parvez**. Opportunities for full-time art education were few. The Mayo School had been founded by Lockwood Kipling in 1875. Unlike its sister institutions in Bombay, Calcutta and Madras, which taught painting, Lahore concentrated solely on crafts. The Fine Art Department opened only in 1958 after the Schools transformation into the National College of Arts. It soon became identified with a modernist international outlook which was actively pursued by its first Director, the American sculptor Mark Sponnenberg. The Ceramics Department was set up by the Japanese potter Takita and **Mian Salahuddin** was among its first graduates; he is to this day one of very few to have bridged the gulf between local tradition and a personal, contemporary idiom in this particular material.

In contrast to this progressive stance, the neo-realism practised at the Punjab University in the Fine Art Department set up by the British trained **Anna Molka** in 1940 has created its own sub-culture of academicism. The cycle is not unique to Pakistan; the skills of drawing and observation of the real world, initially intended to provide girls (until 1955, when the Department became co-educational) with a means of earning a living as teachers are rarely seen as emancipatory. By external standards, these are a relic of the colonial past, especially when employed ostensibly as an end in themselves in realist portrait and landscape painting. The work of the portrait painter **Saeed Akhtar** (incidentally, for many years a Professor at the National College) cannot be so easily dismissed, however; his absolute mastery of his craft is no less a consummate act of self-discipline and self-

Fig **4 Saeed Akhtar** *Girl in White*

expression in Pakistan than it would be in Britain; though for different reasons and with different results (fig **4**).

Akhtar studied in Italy, not an uncommon choice in the 1950s for those who wanted to distance themselves from British influence. **Murtaza Bashir** (b.1933), from East Pakistan, was also there and in his *Self-portrait* of c.1956 created the most confident self-image of this period of internationalism (fig **3**; his name is now Murtaja Baseer). Bashir was one of several painters from the eastern wing of the country who were active in the cultural centres of Lahore and Rawalpindi. **Zainul Abedin** was the best known, having established a formidable reputation with his drawings of the Bengal famine of 1942, and it was he who founded the Fine Art Department at the University of Peshawar. It was an enlightened choice, all the more so when it brought together what were perceived as the country's cultural margins.

Khalid Iqbal's reputation as Pakistan's leading landscape painter extends for over thirty years. In limiting himself largely

30 Ismail Gulgee *Calligraphy* 1999

97 Anwar Jalal Shemza *Roots* 1977

76 Sadequain *Judgement in Paris* 1962

to the nondescript wastelands around the fringes of Lahore, he has created a body of work which evokes a condition of impoverishment only to overcome it through the resources of his own painter's vision (fig **1**). **Khaleem Khan** in Baluchistan and **Anwar Khan** in the North West Frontier Province paint their own regions with equal attachment.

Shakir Ali became the first native director of the National College of Arts in 1961. While his influence may have grown, his own artistic output diminished. The monumentality of his mature style, with stiff figures and simple colour palette, continues his self-conscious primitivism of the 1950s (primitivism in the sense that he chose to focus on the early phases of different civilisations or movements, Altamira and Ajanta being favourites). He wanted to lay a solid foundation on which others could build. The credit generally given to Shakir as the father of modernism in Pakistan was challenged subsequently by **Zubeida Agha** (1922-1997). Her uncompromising individuality was an important example to later women artists; the ambiguous content of her colouristic semi-abstractions established a personal, intimate realm whose value lies in its purity, its very avoidance of the social, political or cultural ideologies through which other artists claimed attention.

Towards the end of his life, Shakir executed an immense mural for the Punjab Public Library in Lahore. With due regard for the setting, the work consists entirely of verses from the Koran. Variation in the colour, size and direction of the Arabic script creates a complex inner dynamic in which individual letters (some many feet high) resolve into units which hover on the verge of figuration (reproduced K S Butt, ed., *Paintings from Pakistan*, p81). It is a dramatic solution to the introduction of art into a public space which at the same time demonstrates the versatility of calligraphy as a visual system which can be genuinely satisfying to both artist and onlooker. The development of artistic calligraphy within Islamic culture reflects both reverence for the sacred texts of the Koran and the avoidance in orthodox tradition of any depiction of living creatures. Its use in present-day Pakistan has become highly politicised, since it was one of the few art forms actively encouraged under the dictatorship of General Zia, when much other artistic expression became an underground activity.

Linguistic signs are arbitrary; they depend entirely on convention and context for their meaning. Yet in comparison with what appeared to be the empty gesturing of much abstract art produced in the fifties and sixties, reference to

calligraphy provided an anchor, a point of contact with common systems of meaning, a potential for communication which recognised a need to translate the 'purely visual' into other types of discourse. **Gulgee** is now the best known exponent of this painterly calligraphy (**30**), with many large scale commissions to his credit throughout the Arab world. The simple requirement to 'read' his energetic brushstrokes from right to left will be an automatic reflex for some, but a profound mental adjustment for others; every mark is inscribed with specific cultural value.

Thus, when **Shemza** began his exploration of the line as a type of writing, he worked with basic forms which were as visually and culturally neutral as possible: the square and the semi-circle. The use he made of this material over many years is a signal of his determination to speak simultaneously to distant communities: England where he lived and Pakistan where he was known and highly regarded. Knowledge of the role of geometry in Islamic architecture on the one hand and his understanding of the sub-atomic theory of the visual expounded in the writings and the work of Paul Klee (which he studied at first hand in Switzerland) were his bedrock. Klee's own indebtedness to the buildings and colours of North Africa made him a sympathetic mentor. It is ironic, but totally symptomatic of the predicament he faced, that Shemza's 'writing' has been reduced in Euramerican commentary to the two letters identifiable in the Roman alphabet, B and D, whereas Shemza's semantics are operating at a deeper level altogether. The *Roots* series (**97**) which he began in 1977 takes the idea of buried meaning as a source of strength and joy, where duality is envisaged as an essential condition of existence.

The work of **Rashid Ahmed Arshad** and **Zahoor Ul Akhlaq** is more than script alone. The character of whole documents emerges as the major theme. The title of Arshad's 1972 exhibition in Karachi, *The Reformation* is indicative of the artist's radical intent, going beyond formalism to engage with the religious connotations of his imagery. Zahoor's 'Firman' series began around 1972. The decorative borders and seals of the official decrees (firman) issued by the Mughal emperors appear as framing devices, but are no more than the trappings of a power whose central message is obscure or absent altogether. Zahoor continued to use the device of a field set within uneven borders, derived from the typical manuscript page as a simple means of locating his work within a specific tradition. This formula was far from restrictive to an artist of his extensive knowledge and understanding, but provided a basis for endless

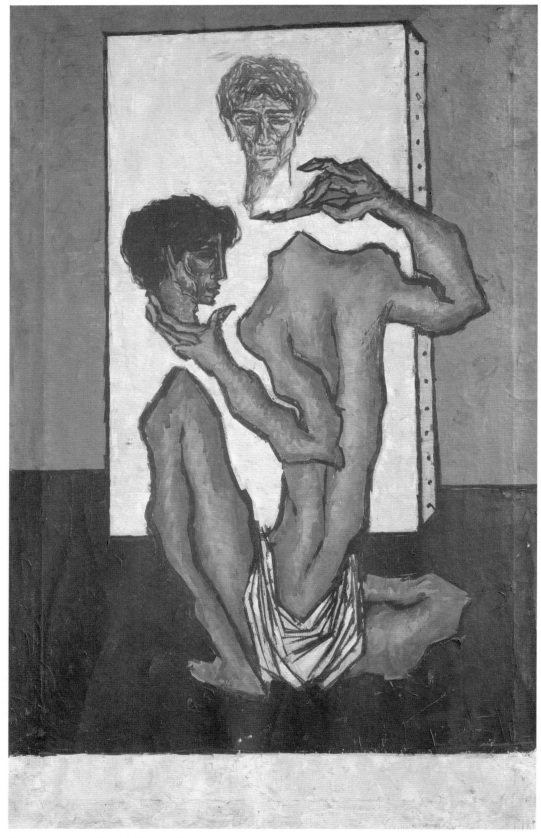

Fig **5 Sadequain** *Untitled (Self-portrait)* c.1966

variation and cultural interplay. His insistence on foregrounding the frame and making it integral to the image is a constant reminder that all art is made and viewed from a position; one that cannot be taken for granted but needs to be externalised and made explicit. Within postmodernism, such a perception might appear commonplace. Zahoor gives the impression that he has long known what for others is a recent discovery. In one of his final series, entitled *A Visit to the Inner Sanctum*, the pictorial geometry defines an inner space that is psychological, accessed through the dance induced trance of the Sufi mystic; there is a deliberate disjuncture between the banal description of the title and the unfathomable realms hinted at by the half-vanishing figure.

In Pakistan, the status of calligraphy and its claims to be considered within the discourse of the modern are unstable. **Hanif Ramay** (b.1931) had explored the notion of the letter as image since the forties, but it was only when an established figure from the fine art field committed himself to the medium that it became of more than local significance. Critics and sourcebooks locate the 'revival' of artistic calligraphy with different artists and historical moments, but there seems no doubt that the person who energised the entire field was **Sadequain**. His *Bull in the Studio* (**75**) is an early example of a string of different personae he adopted; iconoclastic, uncontrollable, he subsumes both Picasso and Shakir (for both of whom the bull was a leitmotif). At the same time, he provides a belated reading of the cubist faceted surface as a maelstrom of scattered sheets which is both constructive and deconstructive. *Judgement in Paris* (**76**) was one of a number of works exhibited to great acclaim in France which appropriate the high ground of European culture while substituting angular kufic script for the human form; there is a 'Last Supper' in the same vein. In 1968 Sadequain created an entire exhibition of paintings based on the lyric poetry of Ghalib, accompanied by calligraphic renditions of his verses; he followed this almost immediately with an exhibition of Koranic verses shown at the Karachi Arts Council during the month of Ramadan. Huge numbers of visitors, drawn from sectors of the population who generally showed no interest in such activities seemed to indicate that 'art had broken the class barrier' (Naqvi, p408). The event proved a false dawn but did give Sadequain a popular status which he espoused in numerous large-scale public projects. *The Saga of Labour* painted in 1969 for the power house of the Mangla Dam, at the time the world's largest engineering project, presents a heroic image of the worker to rival Diego Rivera.

Ever volatile, **Sadequain** cast himself as martyr as well as crusader (fig **5**). The large projects gave his art a social dimension which has rarely been recaptured. The siting of works of art in public spaces has otherwise done little to broaden the constituency for painting. Frequently inspired by an awareness of the exclusivity of most public and all commercial gallery spaces, artists have understandably sought other means of being seen. Many proposals never came to fruition and even those that did are likely to be removed or relocated. The creation by Bhutto's government of the Pakistan National Council of Arts in 1972 and the first national art exhibition held under its auspices in 1973 gave increased recognition to the role of the arts which it has been difficult to sustain in practice; to date, seven national exhibitions have taken place. The relaxed cultural climate which followed the lifting of martial law in 1987 brought about the first Pakistan International Biennale in 1988, but this event has had no successors.

Far from presenting artists with the advantages of patronage and exposure, these high-profile platforms only accentuate their abiding dilemma. The exhibition is not a neutral space, but one where contested notions of the public and private, which may ordinarily remain submerged, come to the fore. The passage from the personal to the collective can in many cases be negotiated only with extreme caution, but it is the paintings, sculptures, collages and prints which act as so many marker posts, to define and delineate a territory whose existence might otherwise go unrecognised, unmapped. **Salima Hashmi's** *A Poem for Zainab* (**31**) introduces a gagged figure to ask explicitly what can, and what cannot be stated. The title refers to a notorious case of a woman brutalised by her husband, but the multiplication of the image suggests that for each case that is exposed, there are many others that are not. Hashmi's stippled surfaces are soft, sensuous even, the reverse of the Warholesque photographs ranged along the lower margin. The body, the female body, its flesh and its spirit, is all tension; neither the self nor the social will provide the looked-for resolution. For Hashmi and a group of women artists in the early 1980s, art became a form of political activism. **Lallarukh** and **Naazish Ata Ullah**, along with a number of women writers, produced uncompromising works on the theme of repression. The legacy of this powerful voice is evident among the very different talents of a younger generation, including **Summaya Durrani**, **Naiza Khan** and **Shahzia Sikander**. 'The personal is political' became almost a slogan of this movement. **Nahid Raza** portrayed herself as the

Fig **6 Jamil Naqsh** *Woman and Pigeons* 1975

sole protector of her two children, following a painful divorce, in a work entitled *Code of Silence* (**73**). **Meher Afroz**, who settled in Karachi in 1973, has made personal integrity a central theme in her work, explored through the physical quality of her rubbed and textured paint layers and the imagery of flaking walls, masks, puppets and fictional portraits which disguise as much as they reveal.

While still a student at the National College in the mid 1980s **Jamal Shah** organised one of the first public protests against the military regime, unfurling an enormous banner along The Mall in Lahore. The very fact of his choosing to major in sculpture was transgressive. He then came to London to study printmaking at the Slade School. To one brought up in Quetta, on the edge of the Baluchistan desert, the unending English rain came to symbolise not only all that was foreign but also the profligacy of the West. The motif still recurs in his latest work as an emblem of flight, escape, 'the Other'.

A R Nagori has long used painting as a means of provocation. The topicality of his subject matter demands immediate attention, achieved through caricature or through vibrant colour, but the effect of the work does not diminish with time; rather the reverse. The images encapsulate narratives, releasing them afresh to the viewer weary or forgetful of former atrocities. While Nagori looked to Gaugin or Grosz, the political comment of **Quddus Mirza's** early paintings is all the more acute for its subversion of Mughal miniature. The ruler in *King with Eleven Fingers* becomes a grotesque, less superhuman and more of a freak. Mirza's work marks a crucial turning point in the use of this material; he looks back not simply for the sake of a visual reference, but also to engage with the subject matter. In so doing, he is keeping in step with developments in Euramerican painting. In calling his harem girl Olympia and layering Manet's brazen nude onto the miniature, **Mirza** turns the idea of source into a polluted stream; one flowing both ways.

In the hands of its recent exponents, both the techniques and the subject matter of miniature painting are being scrutinised. When the older generation used its themes and imagery, it was translated into the foreign medium of oil on canvas and the shift in scale was enough to indicate that Euramerican norms were the dominant party in the dialogue. When first seen in 1971, **Bashir Mirza's** 'Lonely Girls' were shockingly contemporary in their posture and hard-edge manner (**45**). He contracted this strain of feminism abroad, but brought it home to create

Fig **7**
Bashir Mirza
Artist

dramas in which the women's role is still spoken by the voice of a man. A similar ambiguity surrounds the women **Jamil Naqsh** has painted over the last thirty years. His training as a miniature painter is evident in the laboriously worked tapestry of regular brushstrokes or the exquisite subtlety of his superimposed veils of colour and while there is historical precedent among the court painters for his subject of the female nude, this was also, when Naqsh adopted it in the 1960s, an emblem of modernity. For some, the blankly staring eyes and statuesque immobility of these women conveys passivity, but there is also an inner strength, a self possession which has made the Naqsh 'Woman with pigeon' into the presiding genius of numerous mansions of the wealthy in Karachi (fig **6**, cat **59**, **60**).

On a rare occasion when he chose to paraphrase the miniature, **Zahoor** was characteristically incisive. The three sons of Shah Jahan riding to their brother's wedding are varied in scale according to their rank, with the eldest, who is furthest away, also the largest (the miniature by Balchand, dated c.1640 is in the Victoria and Albert Museum, I M 13-1925). This example

Fig **8 Zahoor Ul-Akhlaq** *Three Princes*

of what might be called 'reverse perspective' destabilises the authority structures of Euramerica (linear perspective being just one) which are so often invisible because omnipresent (fig **8**).

The paintings and prints of **Anwar Saeed** are constantly challenging boundaries, wherever he finds them (**77**, **78**, **79**). Some are cultural boundaries, which dissolve in his heterogeneous mix of Hindu, Christian or Graeco-Buddhist imagery. These visual references mask a deeper purpose, one which is more profoundly unsettling and counter-cultural: this is the exploration of the inner self. That he can do this with humour, sensitivity and a textual richness which is lightly handled makes him one of the most impressive figures working in the country today.

Until recently, it was the subjects and images of miniature painting that provided an important stimulus; the cherished techniques, preserved through the execution of copies exhibiting an almost obsessive craftsmanship, seemed the epitome of antiquarianism. Then came **Shahzia Sikander** and *The Scroll* (**98**). The work is a kind of visual diary, a painted autobiography set in modern Lahore; the very shape of it proclaims that the medium is in no way limiting, but offers unique possibilities of self-definition. No longer concerned with the distant past, the work is both present and personal. Her later paintings have continued to develop miniature's historic association with narrative, but the stories are fragmentary and overlapping. Since 1995, Sikander has been resident in the USA. As well as challenging preconceptions about women in Islam, she has used miniature to question the treatment of other minorities within American society (fig **9**). The strong sense of her own identity evident in her choice of medium is magnified when transferred to a foreign environment, but does not preclude engagement with these issues; indeed, it seems to facilitate it, in clearly stating her own position within the host culture.

Imran Qureshi's work is an often humorous subversion of the conventions of miniature painting. Calligraphic borders are composed of collaged strips of newsprint. Masking tape is not extraneous waste, but serves as an extension of the composition. In *A Lover waiting for his Beloved* (**65**) the artist identifies himself with the blue-faced Krishna, sheltering from the rain under a tree. In creating two figures viewed from different directions, he highlights the method of painting, seated cross-legged on the floor, where the sheet is easily rotated. We are reminded that the unique work, framed and glazed on the gallery wall, is a relatively recent imposition, quite unsympathetic to the delicacy of the brushwork and the feelings it portrays. The ongoing *Love Story* series now extends to eight sheets (of which three (**66**) are shown here), a cycle which translates private emotions into a restrained public form.

Storytelling is central to **Fasihullah Ahsan's** painting; his figures are characters in modern fables, trying to find their way between ancient certainties and present-day confusion. **Aisha Khalid's** domestic interiors have darker undercurrents: the patterned surfaces that identify Islam in Euramerica are brought home again, to take on an ironic tone: geometry may not signify order; the cornucopia masks emptiness; drapes camouflage as well as adorn.

The use of floortiles to evoke the home environment in **Huma Mulji's** *One Friday Afternoon in 1994* (**53**) and **Rashid Rana's** chintz-covered artillery shells point to a growing interest among the younger generation in everyday experience (**68**). It is equivocal, it shuttles to and fro between ideas of authenticity and the thornier, less easily manageable realities of family tensions in Mulji's case, militarism in Rana's. New forms and new materials, Rana's printed fabric, vinyl for Mulji's *Proletariat* betray a desire to break free of cosy habitats and explore new territory.

98 Shahzia Sikander *The Scroll* 1991-2

Fig **9 Shahzia Sikander** *Hood's Red Rider #2* 1997

In Karachi, this has meant creating new physical as well as metaphorical spaces in order to open the artistic encounter to different audiences. An installation-cum-performance lasting two weeks in a park in the city centre invited people to contribute their own dreams and aspirations of the ideal home – itself a weighty issue in a city largely populated by refugees and the scene of violent intercommunal feuds. **Durriya Kazi** and **David Aylesworth** have involved the talents of sign painters, ornamental metal workers and truck decorators in a series of collaborative works (**10**). They enshrine the importance of dialogue, a lack of exclusivity, a recognition of other visual and manual traditions which in present-day Karachi are essential not simply to the future of art but to the future of the city.

While **Ali Raza** brought the motifs of truck painting within the formal arrangement of the miniature (**72**), **Asma Mundrawala** takes her popular art neat – or as near to spririt of the original as possible. Her use of Urdu movies finds a counterpart in **Faiza Butt's** *Sexy Still Life* (**19**). During her two years study in London, Butt's interest in folk traditions took an interesting twist when she turned her gaze on the street life of the capital. With the animal prints which are the high street fashion of the moment beginning to appear on packaging and consumer goods, her work questions definitions of identity and individualism in the light of rampant consumerism. **Samina Mansuri** now lives and works in Karachi, but her latest piece was also created in London, during a residency at Gasworks Studios in 1999. Distanced from her usual surroundings, she made drawings which embody mobility, with figures that are individually animated and appear caught in the very process of transformation. The open structure, consisting of sheets which can be grouped in different ways (**43**), and the deliberate intention actively to engage the viewer, reflect her personal situation, but are also entirely symptomatic of the dynamism abroad in Karachi at the moment.

The attention given to work from Pakistan in recent exhibitions in Britain, in the United States and in Australia demonstrates that the particular circumstances in which this art is made do not limit its range: they give it a strength and an urgency which are appreciated both at home and abroad. The urge now is to make work which seeks to establish a common ground, an area of creative interaction which can be about difference without isolation, conviction without condemnation. Is it not time to write off the analysis based on debt, wherever and however incurred, and recognise the riches in which the modern art of Pakistan abounds?

Timothy Wilcox, March 2000

51 Huma Mulji *Heart is where the Home is* 1997

53 Huma Mulji *One Friday Afternoon in 1994* 1998

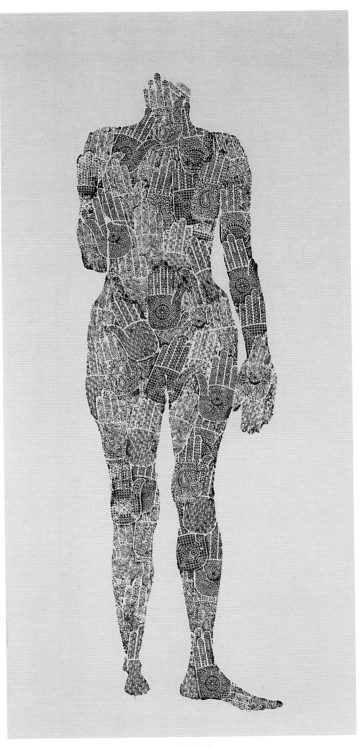 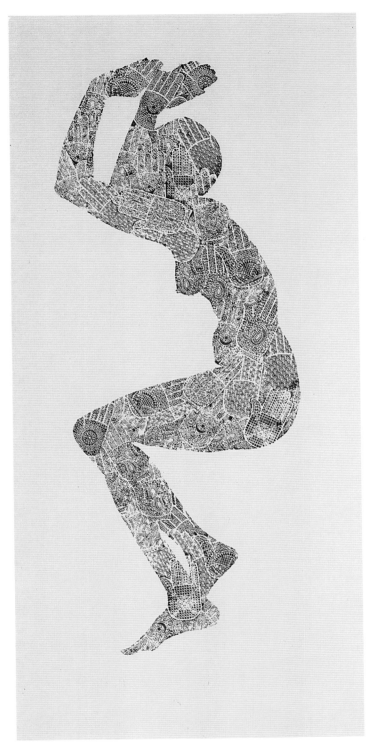

40 Naiza Khan *Henna Hands I and II* 2000

21 Abdur Rahman Chughtai *An Eastern Princess* c.1955

Chughtai 1954

Commenting on his work about this time, the London art magazine *Studio* pointed out that **Chughtai's** work was not merely influenced by Persian and Mughal painting of the past, but it was also 'an avowed re-birth of that art, with some recognition of modern progress and the stamp of individual genius'. It added 'there is an exquisite refinement of mood and method, a lyrical fervour in every line. Effects are economically achieved through concentration on the main theme of the picture.'

That indeed is the secret of Chughtai's fatal charm – fatal to the critical faculties of the spectator – because there is something magical about the working of his imagination, something fantasmagoric. There is seduction in every turn and twist of his drunken reeling lines, as they entwine around one's heart. He depicts life through 'stills' as it were, transforming the particular and the momentary into something universal and abiding. There is apparently no action in his pictures; all the figures are shown in repose, but there is an emotional tension which suggests that something has happened or is about to happen. Also there is the element of an 'unconscious symbolism', several examples of which have been pointed out by Mr A A Hamid: 'Near a very old decrepit beggar in tatters, a spray of brightly coloured flowers is in full bloom; a small bird is singing happily near a woman broken with grief; the hallowed trunk of a dead tree lies near the feet of a youthful and robust prince; two lines of beautiful trees make an arch towards a mound behind which a spotted black leopard is lying waiting. These are only few examples. This unconscious symbolism really expresses the traditional Asian view of life which accepts everything with resignation.'

Chughtai has rarely painted from models; he draws and paints mostly from memory. The artist's scrap-book, in his case, is in his own mind and imagination. This is indeed a double-edged weapon. While it gives freedom, it also encourages idealization and exaggeration. His emphasis on decorative motifs arises chiefly from such idealization. He takes meticulous care in rendering the most intricate tapestries, carvings, garment borders, floor designs and so on. But when it comes to figure drawing, he paints types rather than individuals. His portrait gallery consists of highly stylised figures which have an air of familiarity, but would not answer to a name. His *Mir Sahib* and *The Ambassador*, his *Mother and Child* and *Modesty*, are portrait studies of a culture and an age rather than of the individual depicted. We may admire their grace and sophistication but cannot recognise or identify them. His *Tribal Girl* and *Fragrance of the Valley* are bewitching, but lacking in authenticity; his *College Girls* are models of elegance but transparently unreal. As a critic writing in *The Artist* of London pointed out: 'Chughtai's whole outlook is romantic; he works, as do most Orientals, by rule of thumb rather than observations; he sees through the spectacles of his ancestors, rather than through his own unaided eyes. Everything he touches is a superb piece of craftsmanship. He has almost staggering command of the brush common to the Japanese and Chinese masters: his handling is more akin to the neat and precise style of Persian and Mughal painters. He uses the pencil with the delicacy of silver point in style. The European student can learn much from his remarkable economy of means and material'.

From **Jalal Uddin Ahmed**, *Art in Pakistan, Early Years*
First published 1954, reissued 1964, 1970, 1972

12 Shakir Ali *Still-life with Pineapple and Apple* 1955

Shakir Ali: Painter's Painter 1960

Since 1952, when he landed in Lahore, **Shakir Ali** has been perhaps the most powerful co-influence on the artistic life of this city. Lahore has always been a difficult city to please. At the time Shakir came to settle down here, it had become impossible to please it. It was full of the philistine and the demagogue. The few genuine lovers of art and art-practitioners had withdrawn into their shells or cells, forming coteries where they bemoaned the hard times that had come upon them. They recalled a golden age of art patronage and wished in vain for the fleshpots of Egypt in the desert they had come to inherit.

[…]his early period of painting in Lahore is full of a sense of oppression. The frustrations and hardships of his life in Karachi and elsewhere had made him extremely lonely. He was haunted by the agonising motif of 'The Bull'. The times are usually grey and dull, the masses are splintered and clashing. And in the all-pervading confusion and gloom the only light is the bright ochre symbolic of life and devotion. The overall effect of these paintings is the helplessness of man in face of the brutish element in life. The Europa and the Bull archetype was painted again and again, and perhaps unconsciously, as if the artist were trying to overcome in consciousness the painful mystery of violence.

With *Mother and Child* and *Dove* this period comes to an end. These two paintings signify a reconciliation and return. The storm is over. The circling rhythm of the dove brings a feeling of peace and re-emergence into the harmony of being. The powerfully painted hand of the mother bears a promise of protection.

After this, he did not paint for some time. He became lazy and fat. We accused him of becoming a bourgeois. But he was only hibernating. One day he came to me, glowing with excitement, as if he had laid an egg. He had painted a picture. He asked me to go with him to his studio and look at it. It was a still life – a vase with flowers – in bright glowing colours, yellow and gold and vermillion.

It was the beginning of a new period. The dull heaviness of his anguish was over. Now it was all birds and flowers and men and women, in attitudes and poses of calm and repose. One remarkable painting of this period is *Man and Bird*. The moulding of his figures showed the tender care he had taken, giving an earthly solidity to the characters of his inner drama. Even in abstraction these figures were expressive of meaningful dramatic attitudes. No more did he need to crush and splinter his figures. They followed into one another with a vital rhythm.

In his more recent work one can see an assurance and confidence of eye and hand which is expressive of a feeling of fulfilment. There is no brooding now on themes of loneliness and terror. Abstractions of figures and landscapes are convenient symbols for the vital meaning which he has found in his milieu. The world is peopled with human figures at work or at play. They are involved in the life of the plants and animals and birds and the walls in which they live. The city landscape is as much a part of his active consciousness as the village landscape. *The Potter* expresses the same creative rhythm as the *Musicians in Yellow*. Even the clang and clash of industrialisation is not absent. Pylons express the rhythm of this new element in our national life.

This desire is not an isolated phenomenon. He is not the only one of our artists who has felt lost, uprooted, in a world of incomprehensible conflicts and clashes. It is our widespread feeling – his yearning to belong. In all communities of the world today, writers and artists are feeling limited by the merely forward look, by the puritan desire to belong to a glorious future, because this tendency results in a postponement of actual living. They want to look around and look back, in anger or with nostalgia. Traditionalism, regionalism, primitivism are various forms that this nostalgia assumes among artists. The days of art for art's sake are over. The artist is interested not only in expressing himself, but also expressing his community. Perhaps it would be better to say that he is expressing himself through his community.

Safdar Mir, from *Contemporary Arts in Pakistan*
Editor Jalal Uddin Ahmed, Vol.1, no.6, June 1960

Fig **10 Murtaza Bashir** *Wall Thirty-three* c.1970

Murtaza Bashir 1970

Dialogue with Wall

Even with love I LOOK at my wife, I see WALL
or when
I with my thirsty eyes peep through the thick lens
And SEE my tiny daughter, I see
                        WALL

IF at all I look at my
Father
        Mother
                Friends
I see nothing but
                WALL.
I am in dialogue with the
FRONT
        BACK
        &
        RIGHT
LEFT
Of the WALL
My sight like cold wind HITS
against
WALL, waLL, ThE Wall
And leaves NOTHING but dews.
I, the 13 alphabet man surrounded by the
P r o c e s s i o n of WALLS
IS a PRISONER within it
BUT, NOT MY SOUL.

'I am realist' insists **Murtaza Bashir**, and would not stay for an argument. The latest series of his work called 'the wall', he says, are not abstractions conceived in fancy but recreations of actual visual phenomena which confront us everyday without registering themselves on our perception, hieroglyphics of chipped plaster, the wounds left on a wall by posters ripped off in anger, of ink splashed in fun, lines and marks and graffiti etched out in boredom – and the meaninglessness, the ennui, the isolation of it all – the totality of non-communie interposed beween me and my home, between me alone and my people.

'You can take it or leave it' he says, but that is how it appears to me as a socially conscious artist'. And thus Murtaza Bashir has travelled from the austere linearism of the pathetic, cubist figures in his early work (to some, his most communicative work) through the accentuated pathos of his nightmarish man and bird and fish and cockerel, mostly painted in colours of the penumbra to the designed chaos of 'the wall'. And what provides continuity to this dischord of expression is his perpetual and unfailing excitement with things within and without and the voice of the medium – the orchestration of line or mass or colour as the mood of a particular state of excitement dictates.

'I have done with my wall' he says, 'and am now taking on a recreation of the legendary heritage left by our forebears in the plastic designs of experience'. It is always pleasant to look forward to what he is going to do next.

Faiz Ahmed Faiz

61 Ahmed Parvez *Still-life* 1975

Ahmed Parvez: A Jewel of Pakistani Art 1971

Whatever opinion one may hold about him as a person, one cannot deny the fact that as an artist **Ahmed Parvez** has been creating jewels of Pakistani art.

This fact has been fully recognised in the Western art world. Art critics and connoisseurs of art in London, Paris and New York were deeply excited when they noticed his 'eruption' on the art scene of the West. Since his 'discovery' in 1963, numerous flattering reviews have been appearing in most of the leading dailies and art journals, published from the various art capitals […].

Commenting on his exhibition held at the Commonwealth Institute, the Guardian wrote on May 9 1963, 'There is an opportunity in the case of Parvez of acquiring a work of art of the highest standard for as little as £20'.

This realisation of the greatness of Parvez created such a big demand for his works that buyers began to go even to his flat in London to purchase his paintings. Dukes and duchesses started offering them as birthday presents or wedding gifts to their dear ones.

Newspapers published stories about Parvez with such headlines as 'Painted for survival, now his works hang with Picasso's', or 'The space age artist has landed on Wandsworth' etc.

With fifty exhibitions to his credit in all the art capitals in four continents, Parvez is one of those few outstanding Pakistani artists, who has made a very strong impact upon the Western art world. Today his paintings find pride of place in all leading art galleries, museums and private collections in different countries.

In spite of all his achievements and success in establishing Pakistan on the world art map and winning recognition as a painter of international repute, Ahmed Parvez is not a happy man. His life is a story of constant struggles, endless strifes and heart-rending torments. Scion of a well-to-do family, he saw many ups and downs and faced serious financial troubles, all for the sake of his art. But most of his troubles have been the result of the outburst of his emotions which were sometimes uncontrolled and sometimes explosive.

Parvez is highly sentimental, emotional and temperamental. He possesses a restless soul and is endowed with a rare natural gift of the power of expression […]. That is why sometimes his talks and writings have proved to be unbearable explosions. Some people take his volubility as dramatic utterances aiming at self-promotion. To others his writings project him as a 'talentless' humourist or a 'tactless' satirist. But as a matter of fact in his talks and in his writings, as also in his paintings, there is discernible one common quality – 'the outburst of the pent-up energy as witnessed in the bursting of seed pods, the sudden display of fireworks or the eruption of heavenly bodies'.

The violent and explosive nature of Parvez is best displayed in his paintings and this is also a proof of his greatness. His paintings are the best mirror of his personality. Poet Faiz Ahmed Faiz has rightly described his paintings when he wrote:

> 'Ahmed Parvez in his painting is very voluble and yet withdrawn, greatly excited but very much in control, his effervescence is framed in a strange tranquillity. And these attractive contradictions make not discord but a harmony. This harmony stems, it seems to me, from the close and consistent integrity of his formal exploration, conducted in an equally genuine though variable climate of feeling. All of Parvez's work is imbued with a lyricism, sometimes tender and nostalgic, sometimes violent and protesting, which elevates it for all its decorative and compositional merits much above the purely decorative or the merely formal'.

Author unattributed
From *Artistic Pakistan*, Vol.1 no.2, April 1971
Started in 1967 by Bashir Mirza as a quarterly magazine

45 Bashir Mirza *Lonely Girl* 1971

Bashir Mirza's 'Lonely Girls'

The women he represented in the series were not lonely in the conventional, romantic sense. Nor do any of them look that; rather they are the epitome of those who have taken up life's challenge. 'They are women with definite, separate personalities', says Bashir, 'and because that takes breaking away from society's norms, each is alone in her struggle to discover or maintain her individuality, and therefore lonely.'

They are people or composites of persons he has known or knows. Yet the paintings were not done with any theme in mind. Each was a spontaneous outcome of an association of impressions made on his mind of qualities he found admirable, to be respected and emulated.

Najma Sadeque, *Dawn*, 17 September 1982

Fig **11 Bashir Mirza** *Man and Woman* c.1965

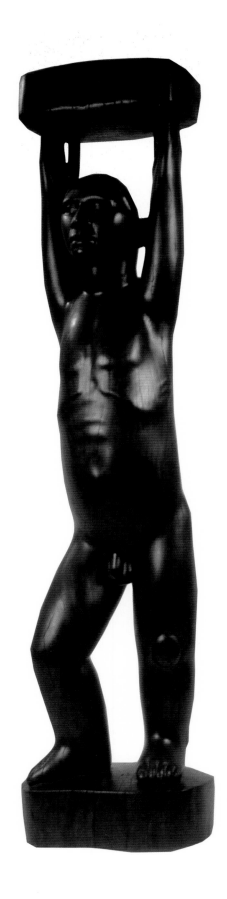

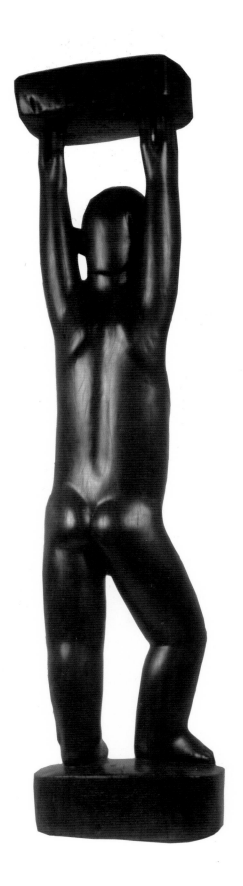

Shahid Sajjad: 'My Primitives' 1994

Shahid Sajjad found his first primitives in the Chittagong hill tracts; those in the exhibition came from the terrain of his experience. In between were wanderings and uninterrupted learning from the wanderings. Together they made the 'janam kundali' of his life and art which are inextricably entwined. His whole life can be seen as a getting away from his world, only to return to himself. He sloughs off his old self as new ones are renewed. This happens because he lays himself open to experience. For him experiencing unconditionally is far more important than seeking pre-conceived experiences. Life and craft are coterminous in Shahid. And this is the only schooling he has known. We live and work without experiencing either. He says, at the height of his career, that it is only now that his concerns are purely sculptural. All along he was familiarising himself with his tools and materials.

If Shahid was questioned who his primitives really are, he would ask us to look at the images he has created of them in wood. If pressed to explain what does he mean by the word, he would reject all the dictionary meanings. Words such as uncivilised, rude, crude and old-fashioned would be repudiated. Shahid believes that his primitives are far more real than the shadows of humanity we have made of ourselves in the name of civilisation and progress. They may not be found easily, but they live in the human psyche. Through his primitives he is attempting a critique of the psyche and of the human state today. Shahid would admit that his primitives are the original humans, people of arrested time and progress. They repudiate history and walk through time in a circle. They are our 'hamzaad's' (doubles). One of our problems is that we have kept them locked in the dungeons of our own self. They have become the troglodytes of Freud, or apparitions of their own primordial mythic beings. Shahid would go a step further and say that they are our contemporaries, perhaps the best friend, philosopher and guide. In the end, he would point to the images themselves and leave us with them, saying that he cannot speak for them really. They came to him and he is introducing them to the wide world [...].

Shahid has not only wandered through geographic and psychic spaces, he has also been a journeyman of craft. He really got to know wood in Rangamati. Fire showed him the pre-historic and arcane secrets of bronze casting. What he learnt, above all, from his experiences was respect for materials and tools and a deep belief in 'tawakkul', very inadequately translated in English as patience. There has to be both patience and trust in this attitude, and even though Shahid would not claim that he is a mystic, his confidence that the next day will add something of value to his experience is deeply religious. A Japanese bronze sculptor, Kato San, whom he acknowledges as his only master, and with whom he has remained in touch, transferred to him his tradition's respect for material. Even the sight of whole families of artisans, father, mother and children, carving images for tourists in Bali was an awakening into the significance of craft as a family vocation. Ancient schools of craft led by masters used to be replicas of Sufi order. Families pursuing the path for something mundane was nonetheless poignant, because craft held in spiritual respect was now a fallen woman selling cheap in the bazaar.

Akbar Naqvi, *'My Primitives'. Wood Carvings 1992-94 by Shahid Sajjad*. Privately published, 1994

left (front and back view)
81 *Naked Man with a Book* 1966-7
reworked 1996-9

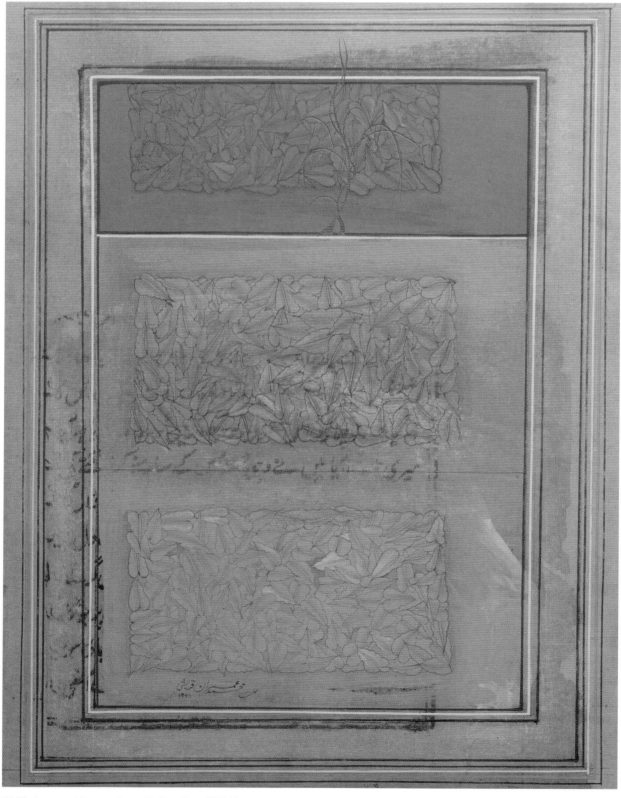

66 Mohammed Imran Qureshi *Love Story II* 1999

Contemporary Miniature 1999

Pakistani painters have always found miniature painting a rich lode of our multi-cultural visual legacy and mined it as a creative resource. However, its emergence as a complete art form with a contemporary ethos can be traced to a movement by young Lahore painters that I would like to refer to as neo-miniaturism. While the miniature painting which resurfaced with new vibrancy in the 1990s was in continuum with time-honoured techniques of painting and substrata preparation, the content had begun to reflect the living culture of our time. This iconoclastic step, taken by the students of Ustad Haji Sharif, delinked miniature from the moribund practices of faithful reproduction and traditional content.

One of the outstanding talents of this movement, **Imran Qureshi**, and his wife **Aisha Khalid**, a relatively new entrant in the field, exhibited their latest works at Chawkandi Gallery recently.

'Painting miniature is like expressing yourself in Urdu' says Imran. Once equipped with the confidence born from the comfort of linking the medium of his dreams with the medium of expression, it released a creative energy that encompasses humour, romance and social awareness with equal ease in his work. No longer inhibited by the social correctness of a naturalised visual expression and the need to compromise on imported metaphors, Imran began to spontaneously weave themes of love and conflict into his iconography. He uses the miniature like a *ghazal*, the versatile form of Urdu poetry, to articulate diverse issues close to his heart. Perhaps inspired by the same tradition, the artist, in the paintings entitled *Love Stories* evokes the tender longing of *visaal* by creating a bed of silken leaves and the serenity of a garden with elegantly foliaged trees of paradise. Its content is constructed from the allegorical idiom of Urdu poetry that measures the pleasure of love in the pain of longing rather than fulfilment. When concerns as a citizen of the 20th century world surface, he paints displaced people and nuclear missiles with their double-edged values of mass destruction and national honour. On a dark tea-stained newspaper heading stands a lone deadly projectile, stark in its bare outline, without the trappings of rhetorical claims. The mirror image of the newspaper headline in the background shows disjointed words 'Ghalat hain', 'mujahideen'. Is the painter questioning how the warriors of Islam are unaware that they can be robbed of martyrdom by this indiscriminate press button weapon, or that destruction by nuclear war can be recognised as the ultimate destruction and denial of God's bounties? To highlight its danger to the plant world a missile slyly nestles among flowers in the monochrome lower border of the painting […].

36 Aisha Khalid *Captive III* 1999

Deeply linked to her everyday experiences is **Aisha Khalid's** art. It is work that is dominated by her love for floral motifs which she enjoys painting and its subtle transformation into feminist emblems. The purdah or curtain that she extensively paints is a multi-layered icon. Not only is the word purdah used for curtain but also for the veil. 'Purdah daalna' means to conceal. The women in her paintings have a tendency to disappear behind the curtain as if to suggest that much of their lives is screened off. The purdah or wall-like curtain used in many middle class homes to create private spaces within a larger more communal space is allegorical of the segmented lives of women who despite their careers are expected on the domestic level to recede behind the veil of customs.

Adorned by colourful floral and vegetable sprays, Aisha's purdah is used repeatedly to comment candidly on the contemporary world's obsession with the veil. She refers in her work to how a so-called liberal Scandinavian nation did not have enough tolerance to give a veiled woman her freedom to work in a public place – a prejudice earlier experienced by headscarf-wearing Muslim schoolgirls in France. Visible is the artist's outrage at the global typecasting exacerbated by the international media's inability to recognise socially and professionally active veiled women in orthodox communities. The world waits for the curtain to finally rise to the reality of their productive lives.

Niilofur Farrukh, *Newsline*, November 1999

Summaya Durrani: A Case for Provocation

Summaya Durrani's works have travelled a great distance from her 1986 exhibition in Lahore. It is difficult to know where to make connections, except that being a thoughtful and passionate artist, Summaya's images reflect her intellectual concerns and emotional journeys.

The 1993 show at Chawkandi makes the discourse on women a central concern. Summaya insists that these works are deliberately 'unpainterly'. The evidence of the mark and gesture have been obliterated and the recourse is the offset litho press. That she has gone to great lengths to remove any overt signs of her interaction with the actual surface of the works implies that the intellect reigns. There is a physical detachment from the making of these objects on a certain level. Her aspiration notwithstanding, Summaya's visual, sensual past is very much present in these complex works. She acknowledges not only this but other images from the past.

Delighting in a variety of visual references, from op-art (manifest in Colin David's paintings of the 70s) to historical stereotypes of the nude, the surface vibrates with lyrical interactions. It is as though there is a tussle abroad, with the artist as both referee and protagonist. Summaya takes up the cudgels on behalf of women, reinvents signs and images, demanding a double-take from the viewer. There is a soft visual stroking here, accompanied by a cerebral nick of the razor-blade.

The unsuspecting viewer is confronted by the works which are obstinate about being categorised. They evade your grasp just as you are about to understand what they are all about. Because, in fact, they are about a lot of things. About women looking at men looking at women. They are about camouflage and counter-camouflage. They are about male-female manipulations, and about the convenience of labels and the comfort of easily readable signs. They are about the seductiveness of rhythm and pattern and what lurks beneath those layers. The layers defy being lifted and meanings mutate.

That Summaya resents her works being 'possessed' as an object is very clear. Her energy is turned towards the viewer, demanding that he or she be made vulnerable.

The works do not offer the cosiness of falling into a 'series'. The painter works hard to delink each work, the viewer starts afresh each time. Here is the female, nude and accessibly framed, approachable. The layers of lace, fabric, pattern, inviting visual recollections. Once you are on the threshold you become aware of the impossibility of taking them at 'face-value'. You begin to understand as you move from one work to the next – so in spite of the artist, the works give up their meanings, not in unison, but in the context they create together.

One is hardly conscious of the fact that there is no colour here. The varied blacks, velvety, tonal and luxuriant, revel in the absence of colour. Summaya Durrani is the consummate designer, she destabilizes the frame and challenges her own expertise. The solutions emerge from the brink. She ridicules intuition and the answers come up pristine.

Many of the works are about the practice of painting and its dialectic. Summaya quotes from Hal Foster in her brochure as a plea for a shift in looking and evaluating art, the artist as a manipulator of signs more than a producer of art objects and the viewer as an active reader of messages rather than a passive contemplator of the aesthetic or consumer of the spectacular.

It may surprise the artist that some of the viewers may choose to ignore the post-modern and will be reading beyond her carefully constructed frameworks. The darker, threatening, more open-ended of her works are most convincing of both her intuition and her and our ultimate vulnerability.

Salima Hashmi in the catalogue *Tampered Surface*, 1996

Catalogue

Sizes are given in centimetres, height before width

*For exhibitions cited in abbreviated form
refer to the* **Resources** *section on page 79*

Meher Afroz

Born Lucknow 1948, India, lives in Karachi
1966 Government School of Arts & Crafts, Lucknow; 1971 Lalit Kala Academy, New Delhi
1975-90 Lecturer, Central Institute of Arts and Crafts, Karachi.
1990- Senior faculty, Indus Valley School, Karachi
One-woman: 1974 Karachi Arts Council, Karachi; 1997 Chawkandi; 1999 Mount Castle Gallery, Colombo, Sri Lanka; 2000 Bretton Hall, Wakefield, England
Group: 1972 1st PNCA National Exhibition; 1977 2nd PNCA National Exhibition (First prize); 1985 5th PNCA National Exhibition (First prize in graphics); 1986 Triennale, New Delhi; 1993 6th Asian Art Biennale, Dhaka; 1994 Bradford; 1994-6 Pasadena
Collections: PNCA; Bradford, England

I treat my work with textures, layers, weathering and seasoning to represent the continuity and passing of phases. The 'Apparition' series has expressed my reaction to the present rat race, which has proved to be a cultural and ideological loss, the loss of values and glorious past.

1 *Apparition Series I* 1999
acrylic on wood, 81 x 41
lent by the artist

2 *Apparition Series II* 1999
acrylic on wood, 81 x 41
lent by the artist

Lubna Agha

Born Quetta 1949, lives in Boston, USA
1968 Karachi School of Arts; 1982 Sacramento State University, USA
One-woman: 1969 Pakistan American Cultural Centre, Karachi; 1973, 1980, 1987 Indus Gallery, Karachi; 1981 Stuart/Scott Gallery, Fair Oaks, California; 1996 Chawkandi Gallery, Karachi
Group: 1973 *Three Non-Depressionists*, Arts Council of Pakistan, Karachi; 1979 Arts Council of Pakistan, Karachi, Lahore, Rawalpindi; 1994 Bradford; 1994-6 Pasadena
Collections: PNCA; Bradford, England

I like to think my work celebrates the nuances of life. Juxtaposed figures and geometric patterns, as well as strong colours like reds, blues and bright cadmiums represent the tapestry of life as I perceive it. The 'Writing on my Hands' series combines the idea of the material (hand) and non-material (the meaning behind the lines on the hands) – the physical and the ethereal, the obvious and the hidden.

3 *Writing on my Hands I* 1998
acrylic on canvas, 40.5 x 30.5
lent by the artist

4 *Writing on my Hands II* 1998
acrylic on canvas, 40.5 x 30.5
lent by the artist

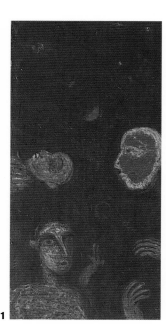

1

2

4

Roohi Ahmed

Born Karachi 1966, lives in Karachi
1988 Karachi School of Art; 1999 School of Visual Art, New York, USA
Group: 1994 6th PNCA National Exhibition; 1995 18th Kanagawa International Print Exhibition, Japan; 1996 7th PNCA National Exhibition

'For me the map is both a literal journey (the safest and shortest) across a troubled city from home to work, but also a signifier of my individual struggle to negotiate my presence within imposed and intrusive regimes of power and meaning.

5 *Dekh Bhaal Ke Jana* 1999
mixed media on gypsum board, 76.2 x 46
lent by Durriya Kazi

6 *Dekh Magar Piyar Se* 1999
mixed media on gypsum board, 76.2 x 46
lent by Durriya Kazi

Syed Zahin Ahmad

Born Amroha, India 1950, lives in Karachi
1969 BA, Karachi University; 1970-74 Karachi School of Art
1974- Lecturer, Karachi School of Art
One-man: 1992 Karachi School of Art
Group: 1980 3rd PNCA National Exhibition; 1982 4th PNCA National Exhibition; 1988 1st Pakistan Biennale; 1994 Pasadena; 1995 Watercolours, VM Gallery, Karachi; 1997 50th Anniversary Exhibition, Art Connoisseur Gallery, London

Once Thatta was a beautiful city of Sindh Province. There were historical high rise buildings made of clay and wood and having a peculiar type of ventilator. A strong desire appeared in my heart to preserve the decaying precious remains through my paintings. Through my watercolours the 'Thatta Buildings' have not only been preserved as heritage they have also become my identity.

7 *Broken Buildings* 1999
watercolour on paper, 41 x 30
lent by the artist

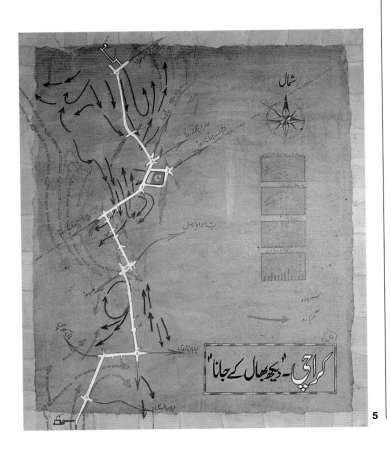

5

7

Fasihullah Ahsan

Born Lahore 1968, lives in Flushing, New York, USA
1993 BFA, NCA
One-man: 1996 Alliance Française, Lahore
Group: 1995 Artists Association of the Punjab, Alhamra Art Gallery,
Lahore (1st prize); 1996 7th PNCA National Exhibition, Islamabad
(Gold medal); 1998 *Contemporary Miniature Painting*, Chawkandi Art,
Karachi

8 *Unexpected Calamity* 1998
gouache on wasli, 51 x 38
lent by the artist

9 *Untitled* 1998
gouache on wasli, 25 x 46
lent by the artist

8

David Alesworth and Durriya Kazi

Alesworth born Wimbledon 1957, Kazi born Karachi 1955, both live
in Karachi
Alesworth 1980 BFA Wimbledon; Kazi 1977 MA (English literature)
Karachi University; 1981 BA (Sculpture) Kingston Polytechnic
Joint: 1995 Indus Gallery, Karachi; 1996 Rohtas Gallery, Islamabad;
1999 1st Asian Art Triennale, Fukuoka, Japan; 1999 Asia-Pacific
Triennale, Brisbane, Australia.
Group: 1994 6th PNCA National Exhibition, Islamabad (Alesworth;
silver medal for sculpture); 1994-6 *An Intelligent Rebellion* (Kazi); 1995
Huddersfield (Kazi); 1996 7th PNCA National Exhibition, Islamabad
(Alesworth); 1998 *Lines of Desire*, Bluecoat Gallery, Liverpool (Kazi).

*The stereotype of the perfect home is invested with a sense of belonging, social
arrival, success, the perfect family, the purpose of enduring difficult working
conditions. Much of the motivation and yearning of contemporary urban life, its
frustrations and anxieties, are associated with negotiations of the home. The home
is seen as a benign, controllable personal space in contrast to the public domain
which is uncontrollable and riven with conflict. However, the outside world lets
intself into the privacy of the home through the media. The idea of the home as
refuge is thus denied. Berger has identified another definition of home that exists
when there is physical loss of home, as in migration. 'Home' then becomes a
routine set of practices, a repetition of habitual interactions. 'Very very sweet
Medina' sets out to create a site for exploring these multilayered notions of home.*

10 *Very Very Sweet Medina (Home Sweet Home)* 1999
installation comprising glitter, perspex, wheels, speakers, lights, stickers,
folders, paper, with: Parvez, cinema artist; Shah, steel house; Sarfaraz,
electrician; Naeem, printer; Sultan, bookbinder; Sheik Chamak Patti
paintings 183 diameter (illustration shows left painting), box 137 high
lent by the artists

10

Liaquat Ali

Born Quetta 1968, lives in Quetta
1989 BFA, NCA
1997-   Baluchistan Community Irrigation and Agriculture Project
One-man: 1998 Majmua Art Gallery, Karachi
Group: 1994 6th PNCA National Exhibition; 1995 Huddersfield;
1997 *Roots of Culture*, tour in Pakistan
Collections: Chief Minister's House, Quetta

At the beginning of each month, by the first sight of the moon we pray for safety, health and the unity of the family and the nation. But the ground realities show a different picture, totally opposite. Perhaps I am dreaming and idealising a situation where there would be no sectarian violence, no starvation. Yeh! Therefore, I pray.

11 *Dua (Prayer)* 1999
oil and enamel on canvas, 102 x 145
lent by the artist

Shakir Ali

Born Rampur, India, 1916, died in Lahore 1975
1938-44 J J School of Art, Bombay; 1946-9 Slade School, London;
1949-50, studied with André Lhote, Paris; 1950-51, School of Industrial
Design, Prague; 1961, Principal, NCA; 1967 Pride of Performance
One-man: 1957 Frere Hall, Karachi; 1960 Lahore; 1966 Arts Council,
Rawalpindi
Group: 1955 3rd Sao Paolo Biennale
Collections: Shakir Ali Museum, Lahore

12 *Still life with Pineapple and Apple* 1955
oil on board, 51 x 60
lent by Wahab Jaffer

13 *Woman with Birdcage* 1968
oil on canvas, 235 x 235
lent by F S and Shahnaz Aijazuddin

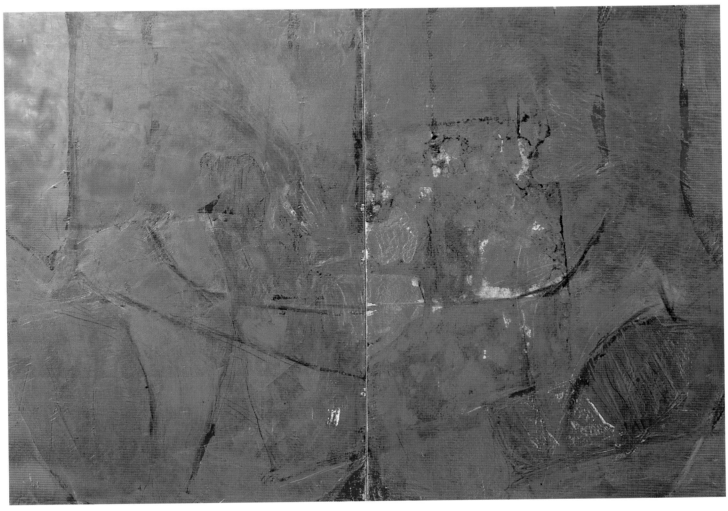

11

Riffat Alvi

Born 1948, lives in Karachi
1973 Karachi School of Art
Art Director, VM Art Gallery, Karachi
One-woman: 1985 *Silent City*, Gallery II, Karachi; 1990 *Moenjodaro*, Zeilitzheim, Germany; 1993 *Lost Civilisation*, Commonwealth Institute, London; 1996 *Dust to Dust II*, Bretton Hall, Wakefield, England
Group: 1979 3rd PNCA National Exhibition; 1988, 1991, 1996 Asian International Watercolour Exhibition; 1988 Asian Art Biennale, Dhaka; 1988 1st Pakistan Biennale; 1994 PNCA National Exhibition; 1996 Birendra Gallery, Katmandu, Nepal; 1998 3rd Visual Arts Exhibition, Ipoh, Malaysia; 2000 Quartersaw Gallery, Portland, Oregon, USA
Collections: Museum of Modern Art Tehran, Iran; National Art Gallery, Harare, Zimbabwe

Earth is my inspiration, it invigorates the spirit of creativity in me. My surfaces are highly tactile, each work a metaphor for an archaeological tumulus; but it is also magnetic because it holds secrets from our past. I am trying to reach the level where the artist devotes his life to catch the essence of things; of fragrance, prayer, manuscripts, lost civilisations from dust to dust, as silent witness, in a cradle of love, at shrines, in fire, on the air, in light.

14 *Unique Vibes* 1998
powdered earth and earth pigments, 40 x 50
lent by Niilofur and Farrukh Sheikh

15 *Kanchey (Marbles)*
powdered earth and mixed media, 59 x 90
lent by the artist

14

Rashid Ahmed Arshad

Born Tihal 1937, lives in Martin, Tennessee, USA
1960 Diploma, NCA, Lahore; 1969 MA Karachi University; 1992 Rutgers University, New Jersey, USA
One-man: 1970 *The Manuscript*, American Center, Karachi; 1972 *The Reformation*, Arts Council of Pakistan, Karachi; 1976 Aldrich Museum of Contemporary Art, Ridgefield, Connecticut USA; 1992 Indus Gallery, Karachi; 1992 Retrospective, University of Tennessee Museum
Publications: *Art in Pakistan*, Erdmann, 1974; *Aesthetic Potential of Calligraphy*, Goethe Institute, Karachi, 1974
Collections: PNCA

Calligraphic elements and other graphic icons appeared in my work following the 1970 show, 'The Manuscript'. They were appropriately titled 'Reformation', 'Revelation' and 'Proclamation'. Apparently, these titles referred to events or documents of historical or religious significance. That may be so, but philosophically these titles are indicative of my artistic endeavours: 'documented', 'reformed', 'revealed' or 'proclaimed'. My aim is not to produce masterpieces of calligraphy but to reveal and redefine its innate beauty in contemporary terms.

16 *Resolution* 1973
oil on canvas 122 x 92
lent by Noorjehan and Akeel Bilgrami

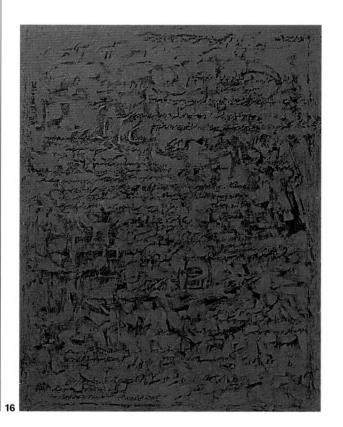

16

Naazish Ata Ullah

Born Sydney, Australia 1950, lives in Lahore
1983, NCA, Lahore; 1985 Slade School of Fine Art, London
(printmaking)
1985 Assistant Professor, NCA; Head of Printmaking
One-woman: 1988 Rohtas Gallery, Islamabad
Group: 1987 *Contemporary artists from Pakistan*, Kunstnersenter Oslo;
1988 1st Pakistan Biennale; 1988 3rd Triennale, New Delhi; 1989 4th
Asian Art Biennale, Dhaka; 1991 *Three Pakistani Woman Artists*, Centre
for Contemporary Art, New Delhi; 1994 Bradford; 1999 The
Quartersaw Gallery, Portland Oregon, USA
Publications: 'Stylistic hybridity and colonial art and design
education; a wooden carved screen by Ram Singh' in T Barringer
and T Flynn, eds, *Colonialism and the Object. Empire, Material Culture and
the Museum*, Routledge, 1998

17 *Fragments of an Allegory VIII* 1993
etching and aquatint with chine collé, 59 x 30
lent by Robert Skelton

Siddiqua Bilgrami

Born Hyderabad, India 1936, lives in Karachi
1954-8 College of Fine Arts, Hyderbad; 1958-60 Accademia delle
Belle Arti, Rome
One-woman: 1961 Jehangir Art Gallery, Bombay, India; 1965 Arts
Council of Pakistan, Karachi; 1991 Retrospective, Arts Council of
Pakistan, Karachi; 1999 24 Westridge Road, Edmonton, Canada
Group: 1959 Galleria San Fedele, Milan, Italy; 1961 All India Fine
Arts and Crafts Society, New Delhi; 1967 Commonwealth Art
Exhibition, London; 1985, 1992, 1997 Chawkandi Art, Karachi;
1994 Bradford
Collections: PNCA; Staff College, Quetta

*External stimuli and inner turmoils produce reverberations in the inner-most senses
and an art form emerges. Movement is ever-present in my work as it is an essential
ingredient of life.*

18 *Revolution and Evolution* 1973
oil on canvas, 91.5 x 90
lent by the artist

17

18

Faiza Butt

Born Lahore 1972, currently lives in London
1994 BFA NCA; 1999 MFA, Slade School of Fine Art, London
One-woman: 1995 Bartel Gallery, Durban, South Africa; 1995 Tatem
Gallery, Pietermaritzberg, South Africa; 1996 Rohtas Gallery,
Islamabad; 1997 Chawkandi Art, Karachi
Group: 1994 PNCA 6th National Exhibition, Islamabad; 1996 PNCA
7th National Exhibition, Islamabad; 1997 3 Women Artists, Rohtas
Gallery, Islamabad

*If art, as has often been said, is a way of imbuing the commonplace with a feeling
of the sublime, then these 'lesser mediums' might be said to be a way of treating
the sublime with a sense of the commonplace. Questioning the political hierarchy of
oil painting on a large canvas, making a material presence and enshrined in the
sacred space of galleries, is where issues in my work emerge.*

*My disregard for the aesthetic and formal conventions of the painting tradition
caused me to rebel against the activity of using ready-made colour with the tool
called the brush, and resulted in the way I construct my paintings. The imagery in
my work is influenced by the evolution of society around me. From the popular
image of a dinosaur to the ultimate fetish appeal of high heels, the inspiration
comes directly from the life I live, the material I pursue and the death I fear.*

19 *Sexy Still-life* 2000
felt tip pens and glass paint on architect's film mounted on perspex,
92 x 70
lent by the the artist

Khalid Saeed Butt

Born Lahore 1950, lives in Lahore
1976 MFA Department of Fine Arts, Punjab University, Lahore
1980- Teaching in Department of Miniature Painting, Punjab
University, Lahore
Group: 1977, 1982, 1984, PNCA National Exhibition; 1988 1st
Pakistan Biennale
Publications: Urdu translation of M R Randhawa, *Indian Miniatures*,
1982
Collections: American Consulate, Lahore; Goethe Institute, Karachi

*Fantasy is an important element of miniature. The artist creates a dramatic
situation. Besides many other things there you'll see fantasised characters representing
good and evil, beauty and ugliness, love and hate. But fantasy in our miniature is
mostly religion-orientated or it represents man's romantic feelings or moods.*

Interview in *The Nation*, 18 January 1990

20 *Scene in Lahore* 1984
gouache on wasli, 25 x 17
lent by Drs G & H Aziz

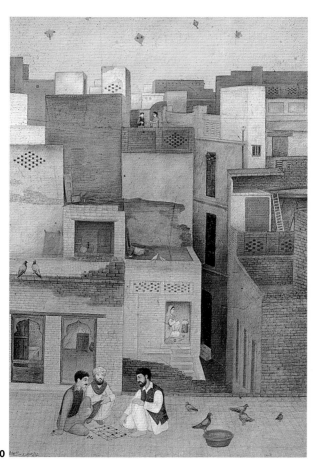

19   20

Abdur Rahman Chughtai

Born Lahore 1894, died Lahore 1975
1968 Pride of Performance
One-man: 1966 Commonwealth Institute, London
Group: 1919 Punjab Fine Art Society, Lahore; 1924 British Empire
Exhibition, Wembley, England; 1937 Royal Academy, London
Publications: *Muraqqa-i-Chugtai*, Lahore 1928; *Amle-i-Chugtai*, Lahore
1968
Collections: PNCA; National Gallery of Modern Art, New Delhi;
British Museum

21 *An Eastern Princess* c.1955
watercolour on paper, 54.5 x 41.5
private collection, London

22 *A Poet with Song Birds* c.1955
watercolour on paper, 55 x 42
private collection, London

Akram Dost

Born Quetta 1958, lives in Quetta
1983 NDA, NCA
Chairman, Department of Fine Arts, University of Baluchistan,
Quetta
One-man: 1993 Arts Council, Quetta; 1994 Rohtas Gallery,
Islamabad; 1994 Art View Gallery, Karachi
Group: 1988 1st Pakistan Biennale, Lahore; 1994 6th National
Exhibition, Islamabad; 1995 Huddersfield
Collections: PNCA

23 *Couple* 1998
oil on panel, 40 x 30
lent by the artist

24 *Nude* 1999
oil on panel, 40 x 30
lent by the artist

22

23

Iqbal Geoffrey

Born Chiniot 1939, lives in Lahore
1958 Punjab University, Lahore (Law); 1966 LLM, Harvard,
Cambridge, MA USA
1962 Huntington Hartford Fellowship; 1963 J D Rockefeller Award
for Creative Painting.
One-man: 1953 *Cultivating Promises in the Rose Garden*, Government
College, Lahore; 1960, Galerie de Seine, Paris; 1962 Retrospective
Alfred Brod Galleries, London; 1965 Santa Barabara Museum of Art;
1968 South Bend Art Center, Indiana; 1972 Arts Council of
Northern Ireland, Belfast; 1985 Arts Council Gallery, Karachi; 1989
Indus Gallery, Karachi; 1995 Lahore Art Gallery, Lahore
Group: 1963 Paris Biennale; 1963, 1965, 1967 Sao Paolo Biennale;
1989 *The Other Story*, Hayward Gallery, London
Collections: Arts Council of England; Tate Gallery, London; Museum
of Fine Arts, Boston MA USA; Pasadena Art Museum, California,
USA

*[Justice], in that it must not only be dispensed but ought to be shown as being
done, evidences a value just short of art in one important respect, i.e. art may
determine to retain oblivion concerning the 'shown' bit. This bestows 'schon'.
Overall the Western conception of art is different and indifferent.*

25 *The {%$^&*(#@~Perplexed} Princess* 1969-99
mixed media, 64 x 88
lent by the artist

26 *Written Piece*
oil and collage on canvas, 61 x 102
lent by the artist

Sabina Gillani

Born Lahore 1965, lives in Lagos
1987 BFA NCA
One-woman: 1991 Chawkandi Art, Karachi; 1991 Interiors Gallery,
Islamabad; 1992 Gallery 306, Toronto, Canada
Group: 1994 6th PNCA National Exhibition; 1994 Bradford
Collections: PNCA

27 *Bright Prospects* 1990
etching and aquatint, 37.8 x 28.2
Collections of Bradford Art Galleries

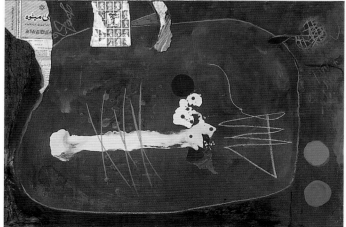

26

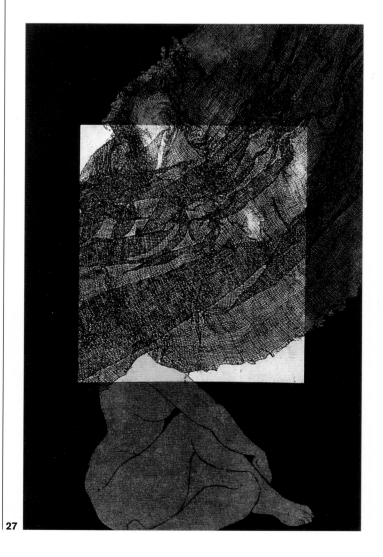

27

Amin Gulgee

Born Karachi 1965, lives in Karachi
1987 BA Yale University, New Haven Connecticut, USA
One-man: 1989 Pakistan Embassy, Washington; 1992, 1996 Lahore
Art Gallery; 1997 Ismaili Centre, London; 1999 Peterborough
Museum, England; 1999 *The Millennium Show: A Search for Light*,
Gallery of the IMF, Washington DC, USA
Group: 1997 8th Asian Art Biennale, Dhaka; 1998 Esposizione
Internazionale di Scultura al Lido, Venice, Italy
Collections: PNCA; Los Angeles County Museum of Art; Jordan
National Gallery, Amman, Jordan; Aga Khan Foundation, New York,
USA

*I work in order to understand myself. It is a highly personal journey in which I try
to discover a balance with my inner self, my culture and my God.*

28 *Father and Son* 1999
copper, bronze and brass, 40 x 25 x 30
lent by the artist

Ismail Gulgee

Born Peshawar 1926, lives in Karachi
1945 BSc Aligarh, India; 1947 MSc Columbia, New York, USA; 1971
Pride of Performance; 1992 ECO Award
One-man: 1950, Stockholm; 1957 *The Afghans*, Kabul; 1979 Arts
Council Gallery, Karachi; 1981 Ismaili Centre, London; 1988 Indus
Gallery, Karachi; 1994 Retrospective, National Assembly, Islamabad;
1995 Commonwealth Institute, London.
Group: 1960 Commonwealth Exhibition, London; 1981, 1983, 1985
PNCA National Exhibition; 1986 3rd Asian Art Biennale, Dhaka;
1988 1st Pakistan Biennale
Collections: H H Aga Khan; Faisal Mosque, Islamabad; National
Assembly, Islamabad

*I am enchanted by Islamic calligraphy and feel close to the Sufi mystics. At the
mystic level barriers melt away and religious experience whether Buddhist, Hindu or
Muslim becomes one. For me, the medium of the unknown is space and the calligraphic
choreography of my painting is the dance of the dervish. To me the act of painting
is the making real of the essential and Yogic experience of life as pure movement.
I live only when I paint. The rest is but a wait, a preparation mixed with prayer
for crossing the threshhold from life to the experience of life.*

29 *Decorative Panel* 1970
oil and gold leaf on canvas
183 x 183
lent by the artist

30 *Calligraphy* 1999
oil on canvas
90 x 60
lent by the artist

28

29

Salima Hashmi

Born Delhi 1942, lives in Lahore
1962 NCA; 1965 Bath Academy of Art, Corsham, England; 1990
MA Rhode Island School of Art and Design, Providence, USA; 1999
Pride of Performance. 1970-95 Lecturer, then Associate Professor
NCA; 1995-9 Principal, NCA; 1999 Professor of Fine Arts, NCA
One-woman: 1987, 1989 *Indesign*, Lahore; 1990 Photographs, East-
West Centre, Hawaii; 1991 *The True Subject*, photographs, Pakistan
Mission to the UN, New York, USA; 1992 Nairang Gallery, Lahore
(2-person with Anwar Saeed); 1992 Chawkandi Art, Karachi; 1998
Chawkandi Art, Karachi (2-person with Anwar Saeed)
Group: 1975 Sao Paolo Biennale; 1986 Triennale, Delhi; Asian Art
Triennale, Dhaka; 1988 1st Pakistan Biennale; 1994 Pasadena; 1994-6
An Intelligent Rebellion, Bradford (co-curator)
Publications: 'Creativity and the Women's Movement' in N S Khan, ed,
A Celebration of Women, Lahore 1995; 'Fifty years on' in V Schofield, ed,
Old Roads, New Highways, London 1998
Collections: PNCA; Bradford

*'The artist's statement can only be randomly evocative about one's concerns which
exist visually. It is always about one's time, its sorrows and its promises, sifted
through the mosaic of images and a myriad of other responses. Defiance, questions,
lyricism, a celebration of life. How does one encompass a fraction of what it
means to be alive in one's time?'*

31 *A Poem for Zainab #14* 1995
mixed media on paper, 55 x 72
lent by the artist

32 *People Wept at Dawn* 1999
mixed media on paper, 72 x 55
lent by the artist

31

Sabah Hussain

Born 1959, lives in Lahore
1982 National Diploma, NCA; 1986-8 Masters in Fine Arts
(Printmaking), Kyoto City Arts College, Japan; 1995 3-month
residency at Victoria & Albert Museum, London
One-woman: 1982 Goethe Institut, Lahore; 1986 Nairang Gallery,
Lahore; 1988 Gallery Beni, Kyoto, Japan; 1991 Lahore Art Gallery,
Lahore; 1994 Chawkandi Art, Karachi; 1999 Okinawa and Kyoto,
Japan
Group:1989, 1991 *Women Artists of Pakistan*, PNCA, Islamabad; 1994
National Exhibition, Islamabad; 1994 Pasadena; 1994 Bradford; 1996
7th National Exhibition, Islamabad (1st prize in Mixed Media)
Collections: PNCA; British Museum, London; Victoria & Albert
Museum, London; Cartwright Hall, Bradford.

33 *Composition (Dancers)*
watercolour on handmade paper, 90 x 60
lent by the artist

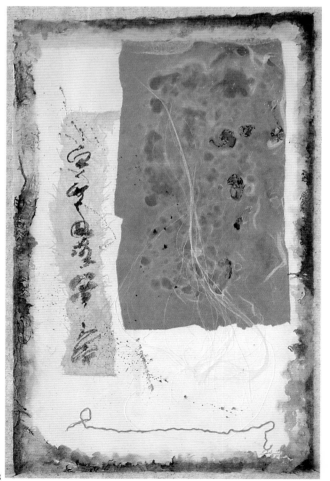

33

Khalid Iqbal

Born Simla, India 1929, lives in Lahore
1949 BA Punjab University; 1955 Slade School of Fine Art, London
1955-65 Lecturer, Punjab University, Lahore; 1965-81, Professor,
National College of Arts, Lahore; 1980 Pride of Performance
Collections: PNCA; Lahore Museum

34 *The Pool (early morning)* 1998
oil on board, 40 x 60
PNCA Collection, Islamabad

Durriya Kazi

see David Alesworth and Durriya Kazi, p48

Aisha Khalid

Born Lahore 1972, lives in Lahore
1997 BFA, NCA
One-woman: 1999 Chawkandi Art, Karachi (with Imran Qureshi)
Group: 1997 Chawkandi Art, Karachi; 1999 *Scope-8*, American Club,
Islamabad

Aisha's works are mysterious, half-narrated stories, suggesting connections and possible endings. Some of the visual references are clear enough; truck paintings, enamel transfers and postcards. Others are more covert and engage the eye with unfamiliar juxtapositioning. (Chawkandi Art catalogue-card, 1999)

35 *Captive III* 1999
gouache on wasli, 28 x 21
private collection, Karachi

36 *Moment II* 1999
gouache on wasli, 28 x 21
private collection, Karachi

34

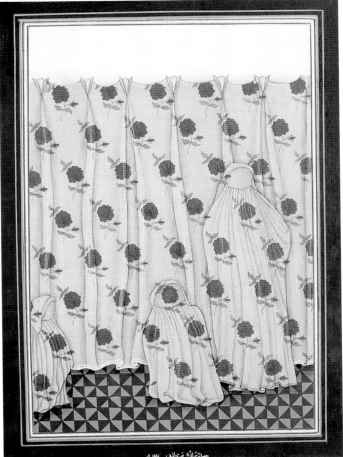

36

Ahmed Khan

Born Shahjehanpur, India 1945, lives in Lahore
1963 Diploma, NCA
Group: 1970 International Print Biennale, Tokyo; 1973-96 All PNCA
National Exhibitions
Public Commissions: National Assembly Building, Islamabad
Collections: PNCA; Library of Congress, Washington DC;
Smithsonian Institute, Washington DC

*We are living in a time-span of at least five thousand years. The bull carts of
Mohenjodaro and the latest cars are moving on the same roads at the same time. I
am an eyewitness to all elements of culture from the primitive to the latest
technology and that is strongly reflected in my work of art.*

*Presently I am working with a new technique, achieving colours directly on the
surfaces of paintings and sculptures from pure silver, with chemical reactions. I am
not satisfied by the illusions of light created by colour pigments; with my technique
I am getting colours without any substance.*

37 *Image of Faith II*
oil and metal on canvas 84 x 84
lent by the artist

Anwar Khan

Born Peshawar 1971, lives in Peshawar
1999 BFA, Institute of Fine Arts, Peshawar University
Group: 1997,1999 S S Haider National Award, Peshawar

38 *Signs of Gandhara* 1999
oil on canvas, 76 x 61
lent by the artist

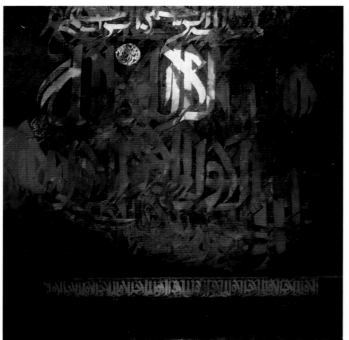

37

38

Kaleem Khan

Born Quetta 1958, lives in Quetta
1983 Diploma NCA
1984 Founding lecturer, Department of Fine Arts, University of Baluchistan, Quetta; Chairman, 1986-94
One-man: 1989 Chawkandi Art, Karachi; 1993 Lahore Art Gallery, Lahore.
Group: 1979, 1985, 1988, 1994, 1996 PNCA National Exhibition; 1988 1st Pakistan Biennale; 1990 *Pursuit of the Real*, Hirschorn Museum, Washington DC; 1994 Pasadena
Collections: PNCA; Lahore Museum; Governor's House, Quetta; Pacific Asia Museum, Pasadena, USA

39 *Desert Encampment* 1998
oil on canvas, 100 x 36
lent by the artist

Naiza Khan

Born Bahawalpur 1968, lives in Karachi
1990 BA Ruskin School, Oxford, England
One-woman: 1993 Chawkandi Art, Karachi; 1995 *La Linea Negra*, Gallery 7, Hong Kong
Group: 1994 6th PNCA National Exhibition, Islamabad; 1994 Bradford; 1995 7th Asian Art Biennale, Dhaka; 1998 *Lines of Desire*, Bluecoat Gallery, Liverpool and tour

40 *Henna Hands I and II* 2000
henna pigment on gesso board, 183 x 122
lent by the artist

39

Nusra Latif

Born Lahore 1973, lives in Lahore
1995 National College of Arts, Lahore
One-woman: 1995 Alliance Francaise, Lahore; 1999 Rohtas Gallery,
Islamabad
Group: 1997 *Contemporary Miniature Painting*, Lahore Museum, Lahore;
1997 *Miniature Painters*, Chawkandi Art, Karachi

*Working on this small scale, the sensitivity of every mark of colour, grain of
texture and its visual prominence is increased; this makes the activity a kind of
sacred and yet intimate process where nothing can be spared or should be ignored.*

41 *…then, afterwards* 1998
gouache, watercolour and graphite on wasli, 20 x 30
lent by the artist

Samina Mansuri

Born Karachi 1956, lives in Karachi
1977 Central Institute of Arts and Crafts, Karachi; 1985 BFA, Pratt
Institute, New York, USA; 1998-1990 New York Studio School; 1999
Residency at Gasworks Studios, London
One-woman: 1997 Eicher Gallery, New Delhi (2-woman with Lala
Rukh); 1997 Chawkandi Art, Karachi
Group: 1994 Bradford; 1995 Huddersfield
Collections: PNCA

*The recent work is about the human predicament as I see it within and outside
myself. These drawings are direct and spontaneous. The tension is beween the
abstract and the figurative. Several drawings work together with no implied narrative.
These abstract/figural forms are animated and don't occupy any specific space.
Expressing perhaps on one level the futility of 'becoming'. The boundaries are open
and fluid, they speak the in-between and the ambiguous. These are dysfunctional
characters, who are barely holding it together or in a general state of splitting or
falling apart. Here identity is unfixed and unstable, these forms are part amorphous,
part defined, and keep changing shape. This is stated with playfulness, humour and
a great deal of sympathy. The observer becomes part of the creative process as the
work does not define but suggests. It aims to create recognition without imposing. In
this sense the work is interactive, and the viewer plays an important role in making
the meaning of the work.*

42 *Raging Eye* 1993
acrylic and brick dust on canvas, 106 x 106
lent by Drs G & H Aziz

43 *Untitled* 1999
pen and ink on paper; 21 sheets, each 60 x 56
lent by the artist

41

43

Jamila Masud

Born Gujranwala 1934, lives in Islamabad
1987 Art Students League of New York, New York, USA
One-woman: 1973 Pakistan Arts Council, Lahore; 1980 National Art Gallery, Islamabad; 1987 Alhamra Art Gallery, Lahore; 1993 *Vanishing Visions* Alhamra Art Gallery, Lahore; 1997 *Chrysanthemums*, Dutch Ambassador's Residence, Islamabad
Group: 1980, 1982, 1985, National Exhibitions; 1981 Asian Art Biennale, Dhaka; 1980 Asian Art, Fukuoka Museum, Japan; 1988 1st Pakistan Biennale, Lahore; 1994 Pasadena
Publications: *Vanishing Visions of Pakistan*, Lahore 1997
Collections: Lahore Museum; National Parliament Building, Islamabad

The 'Vanishing Visions' series features the fast-disappearing urban traditional architecture, dating back half a century or more, of central and southern Pakistan. The idea was both to project the pathos of a neglected legacy as well as to highlight and record some of these vanishing building styles and artefacts in a compelling, yet accurate, style.

44 *Vanishing Visions* 1993
mixed media on paper, 29 x 20
private collection

44

Bashir Mirza

Born Amritsar, India 1941, died Karachi 2000
1962 NDD, National College of Arts, Lahore; 1994 Pride of Performance
One-man: 1963 Nigerian High Commission, Karachi; 1965 Pakistan Arts Council, Karachi; 1968 Pakistan Arts Council, Lahore; 1969 Gallerie Moderne Kunst, Stuttgart; 1971 *Lonely Girl* series, Indus Gallery, Karachi; 1989 *People of Pakistan*, Arts Council of Pakistan, Karachi; 1989 *Hommage to Souza*; 1993, 1994, 1996 Indus Gallery, Karachi
Group: 1966 Biennale, Paris; 1978 Biennale, Tokyo
Collections: Pacific Asia Museum, Pasadena; Library of Congress, Washington DC

45 *Lonely Girl* 1971
oil on canvas, 90 x 90.
lent by Mobina Zuberi

45

Musarrat Mirza

Born Sukkur 1946, lives in Sukkur
Professor, University of Sindh, Jamshoro; 1988 Asian Shield for
Watercolour awarded in Osaka, Japan
One-woman: 1968 Arts Council, Karachi; 1969 *Passions of Mehran*,
Arts Council, Rawalpindi; 1983, 1988, 1989 Rohtas Gallery,
Islamabad; 1999 Chawkandi Art, Karachi
Group: 1976 2nd PNCA National Exhibition; 1980 Asian
Contemporaries, Tokyo; 1986 6th Triennale, Delhi; 1986, 1989 Asian
Arts Triennale, Dhaka; 1988 1st Pakistan Biennnale, Lahore; 1994
Bradford; 1998 Speyong Cultural Centre, Seoul.
Collections: PNCA

*Old houses, pigeons, sun and shadows all contribute to the making of a painting,
amidst them are useen hidden people, their desires, their hopes and aspirations; all
seek the eternal light of fulfilment and salvation. The ceilings of these homes are
floating prayers, the windows are dreams, some lit, some deserted, the stairs lead to
the ever changing battle-ground of life.*

46 *Desert Town*
oil on canvas
private collection, Karachi

46

Quddus Mirza

Born Lahore 1961, lives in Lahore
1986 Diploma NCA; 1991 MFA, Royal College of Art, London
1992 onwards, Lecturer, NCA
One-man: 1987 Nairang Gallery, Lahore; 1988, 1991, 1995 Rohtas
Gallery, Islamabad; 1992 Mina Renton Gallery, London; 1992, 1994,
1996 Chawkandi Art, Karachi; 1994 Rebecca Hossack, London
Group: 1982, 1984, 1994, 1996 PNCA National Exhibition, Islamabad;
1988 1st Pakistan Biennale; 1992 Leicester; 1993 6th Asian Art
Biennale, Dhaka; 1994 Pasadena; 1995 7th Asian Art Biennale,
Dhaka; 1997 Lionel Wendt Gallery, Colombo
Publications: Co-author with S Hashmi, *50 Years of Visual Arts in
Pakistan*, Lahore 1998; arts columnist for *News on Sunday* since July 1998
Collections: PNCA; British Museum; Bradford; Royal College of Art

*My work deals with the images I find in my surroundings. The forms which appear
on walls, the backs of vehicles and on the billboards are our true tradition. I try to
infuse these with a political meaning. The imagery is not realistic on just one level
but a multiple reality, which includes magical, religious and literal realities.*

47 *Olympia* 1986
acrylic and pencil on board,
83 x 60
lent by Salima Hashmi

48 *King with Eleven Fingers* 1987
etching and aquatint,
printed in colour, 50.5 x 34
Collections of Bradford
Art Galleries

49 *My Village came to
Clapham South* 1990
acrylic on canvas, 60 x 53
private collection, London

50 *Hommage to a Man who
is Shooting Himself* 1997-8
oil and enamel on canvas,
140.5 x 182
lent by the artist

49

Huma Mulji

Born Karachi 1970, lives in Karachi

1995, Indus Valley School, Karachi

Group: 1996 *Six Woman Artists*, Frere Hall, Karachi; 1996 7th PNCA National Exhibition, Islamabad; 1999 9th Asian Art Biennale, Dhaka, Bangladesh

The 1997 paintings deal with the notion of camouflage of individual members within a household, particularly a patriarchal set-up, shrouding them in a forced unity. Routine and familiarity sometimes underpin an unrecognised resistance to change and assimilation of the new. Pattern reflects rhythm and repetition; it encloses within its comforting sameness different elements, sometimes contradictory, and calls it one. Therefore there is a reluctance to acknowledge the possibility of its corrosive nature and the futility of such resistance…

51 *Heart is where the Home is* 1997
vinyl, thread and foam on board, 36 x 28
lent by the artist

52 *Proletariat* 1997
vinyl, thread and foam on board, 28 x 36.
lent by the artist

53 *One Friday Afternoon in 1994* 1998
acrylic on board, 122 x 107.
lent by the artist

Asma Mundrawala

Born Karachi 1965, lives in Karachi

1995 BFA Indus Valley School, Karachi

Group: 1996 7th PNCA National Exhibition, Islamabad; 1997 Rohtas Gallery, Karachi; 1999 *Cityscapes*, Frere Hall, Karachi

Ornamentation and the honoring of objects by the use of decoration lend the work an idyllic and optimistic atmosphere, as a means of escape from the volatile world we live in today. Hence the work recreates an unsatisfactory world by furnishing it with imagined alternatives. Personal ideas and childhood associations find expression within the same visual language. At the same time the work challenges the distinction between high and low art. In doing so, it disassociates itself from an established tradition and confronts issues that are vital and pertinent to present-day conditions and influences.

54 *Asli Parri* 1999
mixed media, 22 x 17
lent by the artist

55 *Sona Chandi* 1999
mixed media, 22 x 17
lent by the artist

52

54

Ghulam Mustafa

Born Lahore 1952, lives in Lahore
1974 Diploma NCA
1977 Officer of Punjab Arts Council, Lahore (currently Deputy Director)
One-man: 1988, 1993 Alhamra Art Centre, Lahore; 1990, 1995 Lahore Art Gallery, Lahore; 1996 Kunj Art Gallery, Karachi.
Group: 1996 7th PNCA National Exhibition, Islamabad (1st prize in landscape painting)
Collections: PNCA, Lahore Museum, National Assembly Building, Islamabad

56 *Basant* 1998 (illustration shows left panel)
oil on canvas, 126 x 252 (two panels)
lent by the artist

A R Nagori

Born Junagadh, India 1938, lives in Karachi
1965 University of the Punjab, Lahore; 1970-95 Founding Chairman, and Professor, Fine Arts Department, University of Sindh, Hyderabad
One-man: 1986 Indus Gallery, Karachi; 1988 *An artist's alphabet*, Indus Gallery, Karachi; 1992 Indus Gallery, Karachi; 1995 Lahore Art Gallery, Lahore
Group: 1994 Pasadena.
Collections: PNCA, Pasadena

'My work pertains to the externalisation of 'agony and ecstasy', treachery and turmoil, experienced during the most suppressive years spent during various authoritarian regimes, with or without uniform.'

57 *Legacy* 1996
acrylic on board, 46 x 122
lent by the artist

58 *Holy Beast* 1996
acrylic on board, 47.5 x 124
lent by the artist

58

56

57

Jamil Naqsh

Born Kairana, India, 1939, lives in Karachi
1953 Mayo School, Lahore; 1989 Pride of Performance
One-man: 1962 Pakistan Arts Council, Lahore and Karachi; 1963,
1967 Pakistan Arts Council, Karachi; 1971 Pakistan Art Gallery,
Karachi; 1979 Indus Gallery, Karachi; 1996 The Art Gallery,
Islamabad; 1996 *Modern Manuscripts*, Lahore Art Gallery
Group: 1963 Nepal; 1964 Ceylon; 1970 Galerie Christoph Durr,
Munich, West Germany; 1972-3 PNCA exhibition, international tour;
1992 Delhi and Trivandrum; 1994 Pasadena
Collections: PNCA.

59 *Woman with Pigeon* 1979
oil on canvas pasted on plywood, 105 x 91
lent by the artist

60 *Woman with White Pigeon* 1999
oil on canvas, 124 x 90.5
lent by the artist

Ahmed Parvez

Born Rawalpindi 1926, died Karachi 1979
One-man: 1953 Punjab University, Lahore; 1959 New Vision Centre,
London; 1961, 1965 Arts Council, Lahore; 1963 Ashmolean
Museum, Oxford; 1965, 1972 Arts Council, Karachi; 1968 Gallery
International, New York; 1973 Indus Gallery, Karachi.
Group: 1955 Sao Paolo Biennale; 1973 1st PNCA National
Exhibition (1st Prize); *The Other Story*, Hayward Gallery, London

61 *Still-life* 1975
oil on canvas, 61 x 41
lent by Wahab Jaffer

62 *Painting 20* 1973
acrylic on polystyrene, 35 x 26
PNCA Collection, Islamabad

59

62

Mohammed Imran Qureshi

Born Hyderabad 1972, lives in Lahore
1993 BFA NCA
1994 teaching miniature at NCA
One-man: 1995 Alliance Française, Lahore; 1996 Rohtas Gallery, Islamabad; 1999 Chawkandi Art, Karachi (with Aisha Khalid)
Group: 1994 6th PNCA National Exhibition, Islamabad (Bronze award); 1996 7th PNCA National Exhibition, Islamabad; 1997 Asian Art Biennale, Dhaka; 1997 Draped and Shaped, Cartwright Hall, Bradford, England; 1998 Commonwealth Art Exhibition, National Art Gallery, Kuala Lumpur; 1999 Asia-Pacific Triennale, Brisbane, Australia
Collections: PNCA; Bradford; Queensland Art Gallery, Brisbane, Australia

63 *The Chemistry of what next?* 1994
gouache and watercolour with collage on wasli, 49 x 32
PNCA Collection, Islamabad

64 *Untitled* 1997
watercolour on photo-transfer on wasli 63.3 x 53.2
Collections Bradford Art Galleries

65 *A Lover waiting for his Beloved* 1999
gouache on wasli, 28 x 21
lent by Albert L Borden Jr

66 *Love story I, II & III* 1999
gouache on wasli, 20 x 15
lent by the artist

Shazia Qureshi

Born Karachi, 1969, lives in Karachi
1990 BSc, Karachi University; 1994 Karachi School of Art
One-woman: 1999 VM Gallery, Karachi
Group: 1995 18th International Print Exhibition, Kanagawa, Japan; 1996 VM Gallery, Karachi; 1996 2nd Print Triennale, Cairo

67 *Untitled* 1999
acrylic and bitumen on wood, 59 x 89.5
lent by the artist

63

67

Rashid Rana

Born Lahore 1968, lives in Lahore
1992 BFA, NCA; 1994 MFA Massachusetts College of Arts, Boston
MA USA
Group: 1995 Out of Pakistan, AAMARP Gallery, Boston; 1996 7th
PNCA National Exhibition; 1998 Offset Gallery, Islamabad
Collections: Massachusetts College of Art, Boston MA
Commissions: AD Command Rawalpindi 1999-2000

*In its essence, the deconstruction of the orthodox modern aesthetic is the prime
concern of the work. The vocabulary of abstract/geometric art is reinterpreted by
locating it in the realm of sensuous and readable imagery. The co-existence of
distinct images, layered on each other, in a single work of art, is parallel and an
affirmation/continuation to the dichotomy of visual objects simultaneously
operating in the surrounding.*

68 *Parts of a Desire* 1998
mixed media, object h: 72, painting 135 x 90
lent by the artist

68

Ghulam Rasul

Born Jalundher, India 1942, lives in Islamabad
1964 MFA, Punjab University; 1972 MFA (Printmaking), Northern
Illinois University, Dekalb, USA; 1984-5 Atelier 17, Paris
1974, Director, Visual Arts, PNCA; Joint Director General 1992
One-man: 1966 Punjab University, Lahore; 1969 Art Center,
Northern Illinois University, Dekalb, USA; 1972 Art Center,
University of Illinois, Chicago, USA; 1975 Indus Gallery, Karachi;
1977 National Gallery, Bucharest; 1978 Press Club, Warsaw; 1996
National Art Gallery, Islamabad; 1997 Alhamra Art Center, Lahore.
Group: 1975 Sao Paolo Biennale; 1980 Asian Art Exhibition,
Fukuoka, Japan; 1986 9th International Print Biennale, Bradford,
England; 1986 3rd Asian Art Biennale, Dhaka
Collections: Lahore Museum, Peshawar Museum, Smithsonian
Institute, Washington DC, Bradford, PNCA

*Art is for people. I enjoy the act of painting and leave it behind for others to live
with. A relief from the agonies of life and a moment of reflection.*

69 *Wheat Fields* 1973
oil on canvas, 61 x 92
lent by Lahore Museum

70 *Autumn* 1997
oil on canvas, 61 x 91
lent by the artist

69

Talha Rathore

Born 1969, lives in Flushing, New York, USA
1995 BFA, NCA
One-woman: 1996 Alliance Française, Lahore; 1998 Gallery Espace, New Delhi
Group: 1995 Artists Association of the Punjab, Lahore; 1996 7th PNCA National Exhibition, Islamabad; *Being Minorities*, Hong Kong Art Center, Hong Kong; 1998 Chawkandi Art, Karachi

71 *High Spirits* 1996
gouache on wasli, 18 x 23.5
lent by Salima Hashmi

Ali Raza

Born Lahore 1969, studying in Minneapolis, USA
1991 BFA, NCA
One-man: 1994 Rohtas Gallery, Islamabad; 1997 Rohtas Gallery, Islamabad; 1998 Chawkandi Art, Karachi
Group: 1996 7th PNCA National Exhibition, Islamabad; 1997 *Roots of Culture* workshop and exhibition, National Art Gallery, Islamabad
Collections: PNCA; Bradford

My work is about a fusion of many opposites. Looking into the past and present at the same time and trying to mix up what I extract from postmodern issues with what we have lost in our tradition. Like me, my work is a kind of amalgam of eastern and western cultural values. I consider myself as a product of internationalism by doing what I do; trying to explore the new meanings and the missing links of my identity. On the one hand my work reveals my love of Indian miniature painting and on the other hand it fumbles with the issues of the time, like consumerism.

72 *Not just a Truck* 1997
acrylic on board, 36 x 30
PNCA Collection, Islamabad

71

72

Nahid Raza

Born Delhi 1947, lives in Karachi

1970 Diploma, Central Institute of Art and Craft, Karachi; 1994 established Studio Art, her own school in Karachi

One-woman: 1978, 1983, 1990, 1998 Indus Gallery, Karachi; 1979 Goethe Institut, Karachi; 1986, 1987, 1991, 1992, 1996 Chawkandi Art, Karachi; 1988 Zeilitzheim, Germany; 1989 Anna Blum Haus, Heidelberg, Germany; 1995 Museum of Modern Art Amman, Jordan; 1999 University of Houston, Houston, USA

Group: 1982 4th PNCA National Exhibition, Islamabad; 1988 1st Pakistan Biennale (3rd prize for *Code of Silence*); 1989 Asian Art Show, Fukuoka Museum, Fukuoka, Japan; Asian Art Biennale, Dhaka; 1991 Three Pakistani Women Artists, Delhi; 1994 Bradford

Collections: PNCA, Bradford

The images in her present series look like icons – she uses multiple small divisions akin to miniature paintings which are conceived in the modern perception of the art of today. She is now involved in an approach which incorporates the woman as a whole in ventilating her different perceptions in an all-embracing format. The woman as a person who is determined, strong, with hope, bearing the burden of motherhood, rejecting flesh trade, managing the household as successfully as pursuing statecraft and working as an equal partner with man. Ali Imam, 1998

73 *Code of Silence* 1988
acrylic on handmade paper, 53 x 36
PNCA Collection, Islamabad

73

Lala Rukh

Born Lahore 1948, lives in Lahore

1970, MFA, University of the Punjab, Lahore; 1976, MFA University of Chicago, USA

1978-82, Lecturer, University of the Punjab; 1981 Founder member, Women's Action Forum; 1982- Assistant (later Associate) Professor, NCA

Solo: 1978 Maison de la Culture, Rennes, France; 1997 *Open Wounds*, Eicher Gallery, New Delhi (2-woman with Samina Mansuri)

Group:1993 *Violence*, artist's camp and exhibition, Goethe Institut, Lahore; 1994 6th PNCA National Exhibition, Islamabad; 1994 Pasadena; 1994 Bradford; 1999 9th Asian Art Biennale, Dhaka

Publications: 'Image Nation: A visual text' in N Hussain, S Mumtaz, R Saigol, eds, *Engendering the Nation-State*, 1998

Collections: New York Public Library, New York, USA

One of a series of three prints of the ancient site of Sigiriya in Sri Lanka (AD 477-95). Sigiriya is about memory and history, absence and presence of light and colour and darkness.

74 *Sigiriya: Night* 1993
serigraph and pastels, 22 x 17.5
lent by the artist

74

Sadequain

Born Amroha, India 1930, died Lahore 1987
1948 Agra University; 1962 Pride of Performance
One-man:1955 Suhrawardy residence, Karachi; 1962 Maison de la Culture, Le Havre, France; 1963 Commonwealth Institute, London; 1968 Alhamhra, Lahore; 1969 Ghalib Centenary Calligraphies, Arts Council, Karachi; 1971 Calligraphies, Lahore Museum; 1974 Dubai, Jeddah, Cairo; 1975 Sala Antenelei Roman, Bucharest; State Museum of Oriental Arts, Moscow; 1976 Punjab Arts Council, Lahore
Group: 1961 Biennale de Paris (Lauréat); 1964 5e Salon, Musée de l'Art Moderne, Paris
Public projects: 1967 *Saga of Labour*, Mangla Dam Power House; 1973 Ceiling, Lahore Museum; 1979 Calligraphy Gallery, Lahore Museum
Publications: 1966 illustrations for Camus' *L'étranger*; 1971 illustrations for *Rubaiyyat-e-Sadequain-e-Naqsh*

75 *The Bull in the Studio* 1960
oil on canvas, 86.5 x 115.5
lent by Wahab Jaffer

76 *Judgement in Paris* 1962
oil on canvas, 100 x 49.5
lent by the National College of Arts, Lahore

Anwar Saeed

Born Lahore 1955, lives in Lahore
One-man: 1984 Rohtas Gallery, Islamabad; 1995 Chawkandi Art, Karachi (2-man with Afshar Malik); 1998 Chawkandi Art, Karachi
Group:1992 *Crossing Black Waters*, Leicester City Art Gallery; 1995 7th Asian Art Biennale, Dhaka (Honorable mention)

77 *Love is a Lungfish I* 1992
oil on paper on canvas, 107 x 75
lent by Shakil Saigol

78 *You'll forget love, like other disasters* 1995
etching, 53 x 38
private collection

79 *He knows better than all of us* 1998
acrylic on canvas, 76.5 x 106.5
lent by Naazish Ata Ullah

75

79

Rahat Saeed

Born 1965, lives in Rawalpindi
1989 BFA, NCA
One-man: 1991 Interiors Gallery, Islamabad; 1995 Rohtas Gallery, Islamabad
Group: 1996 7th PNCA National Exhibition, Islamabad

80 *Evening Rose*
mixed media, 61.5 x 74
PNCA Collection, Islamabad

Shahid Sajjad

Born Lahore 1937, lives in Karachi
Self-taught
One-man: 1964, 1974 Arts Council of Pakistan, Karachi; 1976 Indus Gallery, Karachi; 1978 Atelier BM, Karachi; 1987, 1994 Chawkandi Art, Karachi; 1995 NCA Gallery, Lahore
Group: 1992 SAARC Young Contemporaries, Delhi; 1993 Asian Art Biennale, Dhaka; 1994 5th International Biennale, Cairo; 1995 Istaqlal Festival, Jakarta

I want to speak about freedom which, I believe, is the state of my life and work. When an artist is surrounded by temptations from money and success, he has to be free. This is his rebellion. To me man/woman is important for art. We feel that we may have exhausted this image. But we have not. Myths from all civilisations take man as the point where the divine and the human merge. The subject for me is still fresh. In the world today, commercialised, technologised and also trivialised, the primitive in all of us needs to be remembered and acclaimed. This is the fountain of life, the source of life's vitality. My art is not romantic. I am aware also, of the irony that the primitive in us is perhaps doomed. This is why my human images in wood are sad, with the wisdom of the age. I do not have all the answers on this issue and I cannot have them. Only when I work I seem to know what I know.

81 *Naked Man with a Book* 1966-7, reworked 1996-9
wood, smoked, 150 x 34 x 26
lent by the artist

82 *Hostage 4*, 1992-3, reworked 1999
mulberry wood, smoked, 103.5 x 73 x 37
lent by Shezi Nackvi

83 *Vertical Image* 1975
bronze, 41 x 14 x 11
lent by the artist

84 *Vertical Image* 1977-8
bronze, 30 x 12 x 10
lent by Naazi Ata Ullah

80

83

Mian Salahuddin

Born Kasur 1938, lives in Lahore
1962 Diploma NCA; 1966 Cranbrook Academy, Michigan, USA
1963-98 Lecturer in ceramics, NCA
One-man: 1970 The Gallery, Karachi; 1971 American Centre, Lahore;
1982 *Ceramics, Enamels, Weavings*, Rohtas Gallery, Rawalpindi; 1985, 1987,
1990, 1992 Chawkandi Art, Karachi; 1997 Kunj Gallery, Karachi.
Group: 1971, 1973 Biennale di Ceramica, Faenza, Italy; 1982 4th
PNCA National Exhibition, Islamabad (1st prize in ceramics)

85 *Animal* c.1992-3
stoneware, h:15.5
lent by Drs G & H Aziz

86 *Animal* c.1992-3
stoneware, h:17.5.
lent by Drs G & H Aziz

87 *Animal* c.1992-3
stoneware, h:11.
lent by Noorjehan and Akeel Bilgrami

88 *Animal* c.1992-3
stoneware, h:20.
lent by Noorjehan and Akeel Bilgrami

89 *Animal* c.1999
stoneware, h:10.5.
private collection

Unver Shafi

Born Karachi 1961, lives in Karachi
1984 BA (English literature), Kenyon College USA
Solo: 1986 Indus Gallery; 1987 Rohtas Gallery, Islamabad; 1987,
1994, 1996, 1998 Alhamra Art Gallery, Lahore; 1990, 1991 Ziggurat
Gallery, Karachi; 1992 French Embassy, Islamabad; 1995 Indus
Gallery; 1995 Rohtas Gallery, Islamabad; 1997 Chawkandi Art,
Karachi
Group: 1994 4th Asian Art Exhibition, Fukuoka Art Museum,
Fukuoka, Japan; 1996 7th PNCA National Exhibition, Islamabad
(Painting prize)
Collections: PNCA; Commonwealth Institute, London

90 *Dinner at DI (After Dinner in a French Restaurant)* 1992
oil on canvas, 121.8 x 89
lent by Naeem Pasha

85,86

90

Jamal Shah

Born Quetta 1956, lives in Islamabad
1978 MA, English literature, Baluchistan University; 1983 NCA;
1988 MFA, Slade School of Fine Art, London (printmaking)
One-man: 1992, 1996 Lahore Art Gallery, Lahore
Group: 1994 4th Asian Art Exhibition, Fukuoka Museum, Japan
Collections: PNCA; Victoria and Albert Museum; Fukuoka
Museum, Japan

*My recent work is about the frozen moments when you feel free within your cage
and wish to prolong this forever, knowing very well the feeling will pass the next
moment. The work is also about exploring a new vocabulary, a personal one.*

91 *A Staged Reception and a little bit of Rain* 1988
etching, 106 x 75
lent by Rita Donagh

92 *A Figure Contemplating* 1988
etching, 50 x 66
lent by Rita Donagh

93 *Dreamer* 1999
oil on wood, 152.5 x 91.5
lent by Albert L Borden Jr

93

Tehmina Shah

Born Lahore 1966, lives in London
1988 BFA, NCA; 1989 MA (Printmaking), Chelsea School of Art,
London
One-woman: 1995 Croydon Clocktower; 1999 Art Rium Gallery,
Germany
Group: 1991 *A Table for Four*, Bluecoat Gallery, Liverpool; 1992 Black
Arts Gallery, Finsbury Park, London; 1994 Mead Gallery, Warwick
University; 1994 Bradford

*My intention is to involve the viewer in a creative process of constructing meaning.
The sense of my story lies in ambiguity, in many layers, going back to early
childhood fantasies and forward to many dreams and experiences as an adult. Keep
a door open on mystery and invent stories through this conjecture of aspects (images
within images), forms which are created or which will exist in accordance with the
state of mind of the spectator.*

94 *Calligraphic Tiger* 1993
etching with handpainting, 31.5 x 24
Collections of Bradford Art Galleries

94

73

Anwar Jalal Shemza

Born Simla, India 1928, died Stafford, England 1985
1947 Diploma, Mayo School of Art, Lahore; 1959 Diploma, Slade
School, London
One-man: 1959 New Vision Centre, London; 1960 Gallery One,
London; 1960 Pakistan Arts Council, Lahore; 1963 Gulbenkian
Museum of Oriental Art Durham; 1964 Ashmolean Museum, Oxford;
1966 Commonwealth Institute, London; 1967 Pakistan Arts Council,
Lahore; 1972 Ashmolean Museum, Oxford; 1985 Memorial Exhibition,
Lahore, Islamabad, Rawalpindi; 1997 City Art Gallery, Birmingham
Group: 1961 *Mostra di pittura Pakistana contemporanea*, Milan, Italy; 1962,
1964, 1968 International Print Biennale, Tokyo; 1965 2nd
Commonwealth Biennale of Abstract Art, Commonwealth Institute,
London; 1965 International Biennial of Young Artists, Paris; 1986
Triennale, Delhi; 1989 *The Other Story*, Hayward Gallery, London
Collections: PNCA; Albertina, Vienna; Ashmolean Museum, Oxford;
Wolverhampton Art Gallery

*My work is based on the simplification of three-dimensional, solid, architectural
reality and on the decorative elements of calligraphy.*

95 *The Wall* 1958
oil on board 61 x 46
lent by Birmingham City Museum & Art Gallery

96 *Love Letter* 1962
oil on hand dyed cotton on board, 76 x 56
lent by Mary Shemza

97 *Roots* 1977
oil on hand dyed cotton on board, 74 x 54
lent by Mary Shemza

95

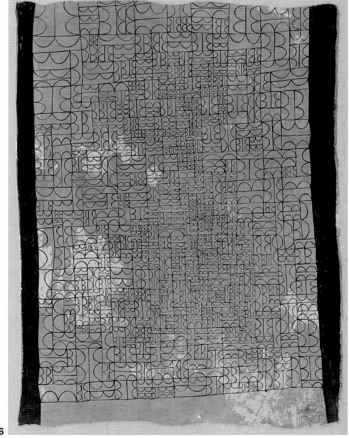

96

Shahzia Sikander

Born Lahore 1969, lives in Houston and New York USA
1992 BFA, NCA (Shakir Ali Award); 1994 MFA Rhode Island School of Design, Providence,Rhode Island, USA
One-woman: 1993, Pakistan Embassy, Washington DC; 1994 *Veil: In their minds and on our heads*, Sol Koffler, Rhode Island School of Design, Providence RI, USA; 1998 The Renaissance Society at the University of Chicago; 1998 The Kemper Museum of Contemporary Art and Design, Kansas City MO USA; 1999 *Directions*, Hirschhorn Museum and Sculpture Garden, Washington DC; 2000 Whitney Museum, New York
Group: 1994 Pasadena; 1994 Bradford; 1999 *The American Century*, Whitney Museum, New York; 1999 *Art worlds in dialogue*, Ludwig Museum, Köln, Germany.
Collections: Bradford; Olympic Museum, Switzerland; Whitney Museum, New York

98 *The Scroll* 1991-2 (illustration shows detail)
vegetable colour, dry pigment and watercolour on wasli, 85 x 412
lent by the artist

Tasadaq Sohail

Born Jullunder, India 1930, lives in London
One-man: 1976 Heatherdon Gallery, London; 1977, 1985, 1986, 1989, 1991, 1993, 1994, 1996, 1998 Indus Gallery, Karachi; 1979 October Gallery, London; 1991 South Bank Centre, London; 1993 Art Heritage, New Delhi.
Collections: PNCA; Arts Council of England; Victoria and Albert Museum

99 *The World of Storytellers, Liars and Hypocrites* 1993
oil on canvas, 35.5 x 30
lent by Louise Zewig

In my youth I was fascinated by the Persian writer Saadie's fables, they were very very short like children's stories but big messages for big big problems. I wanted to say those things in painting. Because painting is the international language but my paintings are not as straight forward as they look; those critics who think they are what they look are wrong.

98

99

Masooma Syed

Born Lahore 1971, lives in Lahore
1994 BFA NCA
1998 Visiting lecturer, NCA
One-woman: 1995 Rohtas Gallery, Islamabad; 1997 College of Fine
Arts, University of New South Wales, Sydney, Australia
Group: 1994 *Women Artists*, Alhamra Art Centre, Lahore; 1994 4th
PNCA National Exhibition, Islamabad; 1995 Pakistani Artists, Cairo,
Damascus, Oman
Collections: PNCA

*…a flow of fragmented ideas, mnemonic images and time-free associations,
contradictions and juxtapositions. The idea is to hold the mind in suspension across
the field of possibilities rather than to arrest it in a concept.*

*I see my work depicting various moods in a playful manner. To me it is a
purposeful, delicate quest for the naïve or truth.*

100 *Untitled* 1995
mixed media on aluminium sheet, 94 x 88
private collection

Zahoor Ul Akhlaq

Born New Delhi 1941, died Lahore 1999
1962 Diploma NCA; 1969 Hornsey College of Art, London; 1989
post-doctoral studies at Yale University, New Haven, USA
1962-94 lecturer, NCA
One-man: 1993 Museum of Painting and Sculpture, Ankara, Turkey;
1995 *Out of Pakistan*, Northeastern University, Boston, USA; 1997
NCA, Lahore; 1998 Indus Valley School, Karachi
Group: 1994 Pasadena; 1997 *Modernities and Memories*, Venice Biennale
Collections: PNCA; Bibliotheque National, Paris; Hiroshima
Museum, Japan; National Museum, Amman

*The act of painting is one of the ways to manifest, adorn and celebrate the
experience of life in its gaiety and pain. For me it is a necessity to excavate, unravel
and recompose the contextual iconography of being. 'A visit to the inner sanctum' is
a series that relates man to man, and the man to the environment. It is not a
comment or a description, it is just a page from a scrapbook noting things from the
past and the present. The process of living initiates a mode of expression in
sharing with things past and present in day-to-day existence.' 1997*

100

102

101 *Notes III* 1990
acrylic on wood, 33 x 24
lent by Noorjehan and Akeel Bilgrami

102 *Notes IV* 1990
acrylic on wood, 33 x 24
lent by Noorjehan and Akeel Bilgrami

103 *A Visit to the Inner Sanctum* 1997
acrylic on canvas 229 x 168
lent by Sheherezade Alam and Nurjahan Akhlaq

104 *A Visit to the Inner Sanctum* 1997
acrylic on canvas 229 x 168
lent by Sheherezade Alam and Nurjahan Akhlaq

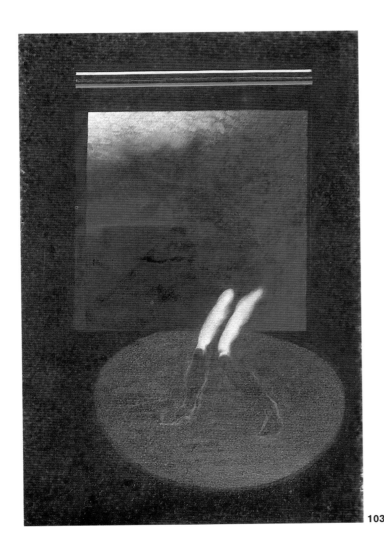

103

104

Ijaz Ul Hassan

Born Lahore 1940, lives in Lahore

1961-2 St Martins School of Art, London; 1966 MA (English) St John's College Cambridge, England; 1993 Pride of Performance

One-man: 1992 Lahore Art Gallery

Publications: *Painting in Pakistan*, Ferrozsons, Lahore 1990

Collections: PNCA, Lahore Art Gallery; Fukuoka Museum, Fukuoka, Japan

105 *Garden and Door*
oil on canvas, 155 x 47
lent by Wahab Jaffer

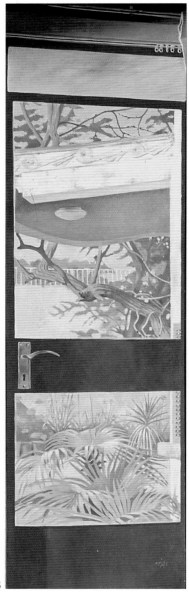

105

List of Figures

Resources

Books: General

Clark, John	*Modernity in Asian Art.* Wild Peony Press, Sydney, 1993
Clark, John	*Modern Asian Art.* University of Hawaii Press, Honolulu, 1998
Schofield, V, ed.	*Old Roads, New Highways; Fifty Years of Pakistan.* Oxford University Press, Karachi, 1997

Books: Art in Pakistan

Ahmed, Jalaluddin	*Art in Pakistan: Early Years.* 1954, reprinted Kegan Paul, Trench & Co, London 1972
Ali, Amjad	*Painters of Pakistan.* National Book Foundation, Islamabad, 1997
Arts & the Islamic World	*50 Years of Art in Pakistan.* Special Volume, Arts & the Islamic World, no.32. Islamic Arts Foundation, London 1997
Butt, K S, ed.	*Paintings from Pakistan.* Idara Saqafat-e-Pakistan, Islamabad, 1988
Farrukh, Niilofur	*Pioneering Perspectives.* Ferozsons, Lahore, 1998
Hashmi, Salima with Quddus Mirza	*50 Years of Visual Arts in Pakistan.* PNCA, Islamabad, 1997
Hassan, Musarrat	*Painting in the Punjab Plains.* Ferozsons, Lahore, 1998
Naqvi, Akbar	*Image and Identity. Fifty years of Painting and Sculpture in Pakistan.* Oxford University Press, Karachi, 1998
Sirhandi, Marcella N	*Contemporary Painitng in Pakistan.* Ferozsons, Lahore, 1992
Ul Hassan, Ijaz	*Painting in Pakistan.* Ferozsons, Lahore, 1991

Exhibition Catalogues

Bradford 1994	*An Intelligent Rebellion. Women Artists of Pakistan.* Cartwright Hall, Bradford 1994 (catalogue by Salima Hashmi and N Poovaya-Smith)
Brisbane 1999	3rd Asia Pacific Triennale. Queensland Art Gallery, Brisbane, 1999
Colombo 1997	*'Rumours of Spring'; Eight Contemporary Artists from Pakistan.* Lionel Wendt Art Gallery, Colombo 1997 (curated by Z ul Aklaq)
Fukuoka 1994	*Realism As an Attitude.* 4th Asian Art Show 1994. Fukuoka Art Museum, 1994 (includes 'Women Artists in the Muslim World' by S Hashmi)
Fukuoka 1999	5th Asian Art Show 1999. Fukuoka Art Museum, 1999
Leicester 1992	*Crossing Black Waters.* City Art Gallery, Leicester, 1992 (catalogue ed. A de Souza and S Merali)
London 1989	*The Other Story. Afro-Asian Artists in Post-war Britain.* Hayward Gallery, London 1989 (catalogue by Rasheed Araeen)
Huddersfield 1995	*Tampered Surface. Six Artists from Pakistan.* Huddersfield Art Gallery 1995 (curated by Alnoor Mitha and Richard Hylton)
Pasadena 1994	*A Selection of Contemporary Paintings from Pakistan.* Pacific Asia Museum, Pasadena CA 1994 (catalogue by M Nesom Sirhandi)
Washington 1999	*Directions: Shahzia Sikander.* Hirschhorn Museum & Sculpture Garden, Smithsonian Institution, Washington DC, 1999 (catalogue by V Fletcher)

CD-Rom

	Pakistan: 50 Years. An Art Retrospective. ABN-AMRO Bank, Karachi, 1997

Acknowledgements

Pakistan: Another Vision has been a collaborative venture involving a large number of individuals and organisations in Britain and in Pakistan. We are grateful to the Pakistan National Council of Arts for its invaluable support, both practical and financial; to its Director General, Ghulam Rasul and its regional officers, Ghulam Mustafa in Lahore, Shamim Alam and Ghias-ud-din Asfar in Karachi; and also to Jehanzeb Malik and Iqbal Awan of the Abasin Arts Council in Peshawar and Abdullah Baluch of the Baluchistan Arts Council in Quetta, whose legendary hospitality surpassed all expectations. The development and final shape of the project owe much to the generosity of many artists, critics, collectors and gallery owners in Pakistan; we are indebted to the free contribution of knowledge and advice from Professor Salima Hashmi, Dr Akbar Naqvi, Ijaz ul Hassan, Riffat Alvi, Naazish Ata Ullah, Nasim Akhtar, John Cowasji, Niilofur Farrukh, Marjorie Hussain, Ali Imam, Quddus Mirza, Naeem Pasha, Nahid Raza, Sajida Vandal and Mobina Zuberi. Dr Marcella Nesom Sirhandi made available part of her research archive, which has greatly enhanced the small anthology section included here. The experience of Zohra Hussain at the Chawkandi Gallery in Karachi proved invaluable on many counts.

In Britain, we are grateful for the good counsel of the exhibition's Advisory Committee, Sir Nicholas Barrington (Chairman), Rachel Abedi, Alistair Duncan, Baroness Flather, Mumtaz Hasan Khan, Nima Poovaya-Smith and Soni Zuberi-Shah; Shahnaz Hamid and Hamid Khan of the Pakistan High Commission; and especially John Holt and Robert Skelton. Zafar Malik, Managing Editor of *Arts & The Islamic World* made many of the initial contacts in Pakistan and acted as an important catalyst as the exhibition proposal became a reality. Sara Riaz Khan has given the project precious administrative support and Anita Chowdry created an imaginative community education programme.

At SOAS, Giles Tillotson and John Hollingworth have been sympathetic and dedicated hosts; for the UK tour, it has been a pleasure to collaborate with Jon Benington, Jenny Hall, Robert Hall, Alnoor Mitha and Cheryl Cooper. The exhibition's designers, Allan Parker for graphics and Jeremy Brook for the catalogue, have captured the work's remarkable range with great skill and understanding. Finally, we record again our enormous gratitude to all the artists in Pakistan, as well as in Britain and in the USA, for their participation. It is they who have enabled us to embody our ambition to see **Pakistan: Another Vision**.

Katriana Hazell, Cultural Director, Asia House
Timothy Wilcox, Curator